I0093891

ISEAS
perspective

WATCHING THE INDONESIAN
ELECTIONS 2014

ISEAS Perspective

Editorial Chairman	Tan Chin Tiong
Managing Editor	Ooi Kee Beng
Production Editors	Benjamin Loh Su-Ann Oh Lee Poh Onn
Editorial Committee	Terence Chong Francis E. Hutchinson Daljit Singh

The **Institute of Southeast Asian Studies (ISEAS)** was established as an autonomous organization in 1968. It is a regional centre dedicated to the study of socio-political, security and economic trends and developments in Southeast Asia and its wider geostrategic and economic environment. The Institute's research programmes are the Regional Economic Studies (RES, including ASEAN and APEC), Regional Strategic and Political Studies (RSPS), and Regional Social and Cultural Studies (RSCS).

ISEAS Publishing, an established academic press, has issued more than 2,000 books and journals. It is the largest scholarly publisher of research about Southeast Asia from within the region. ISEAS Publishing works with many other academic and trade publishers and distributors to disseminate important research and analyses from and about Southeast Asia to the rest of the world.

ISEAS
perspective

WATCHING THE INDONESIAN
ELECTIONS 2014

EDITED BY
ULLA FIONNA

ISEAS
INSTITUTE OF SOUTHEAST ASIAN STUDIES
Singapore

First published in Singapore in 2015 by
ISEAS Publishing
Institute of Southeast Asian Studies
30 Heng Mui Keng Terrace
Pasir Panjang
Singapore 119614

E-mail: publish@iseas.edu.sg
Website: http://bookshop.iseas.edu.sg

The responsibility for facts and opinions in this publication rests exclusively with the authors and their interpretations do not necessarily reflect the views or the policy of the publishers or their supporters.

ISEAS Library Cataloguing-in-Publication Data

ISEAS Perspective.
  Watching the Indonesian Elections 2014 / editor, Ulla Fionna.
  1. Presidents—Indonesia—Election—2014.
  2. Indonesia. Dewan Perwakilan Rakyat—Elections, 2014.
  3. Elections—Indonesia.
  4. Joko Widodo, 1961–
  5. Indonesia—Politics and government—1998–
  I. Ulla Fionna.
  II. Title.
JQ778 I59   2015

ISBN 978-981-4620-83-3 (soft cover)
ISBN 978-981-4620-84-0 (e-book, PDF)

Cover photo: Indonesian front runner presidential candidate Joko Widodo addresses supporters during a campaign rally in Jakarta on 26 June 2014.
Credit: Romeo Gacad/AFP/Getty Images

Typeset by Superskill Graphics Pte Ltd
Printed in Singapore by Markono Print Media Pte Ltd

CONTENTS

FOREWORD

ISEAS Perspective was quietly started in the middle of 2013. This series of analytical briefs on Southeast Asian current affairs thus came into being around the same time that the Indonesia Studies Programme was revamped at the Institute.

Already then, the signs were already clear that the Indonesian elections scheduled for 2014 were going to be very significant ones, as a window not only into how the country had been developing since the fall of Suharto in 1998 but also into how the democratization process in the country begun in all earnestness in 2008 had been faring.

In the weeks before, during and after the elections, Indonesia experts based at or otherwise affiliated to ISEAS, were sent out on fieldwork trips to sharpen their sense of what the most profound changes and the most significant trends occurring in Indonesia were; and to write reports on the current state of this giant archipelagic country.

Their findings were made public through *ISEAS Perspective*. A series of well-attended seminars were also arranged at the Institute throughout the period. Events were moving quickly though, and the publishing schedule could not always keep up with changes on the ground, nor with the number of articles submitted. Of the eighteen articles written, only fifteen saw immediate light of day.

This compilation allows for the remaining three to be published for the first time. As a collection, the articles provide anyone interested in Indonesia — and given the prominence of this country, that should include anyone interested in Southeast Asia and East Asia — with an effective introduction to the country's present social, economic and political situation.

The election of Joko Widodo as President in itself robustly challenges the status quo of established political parties and traditional power holders, and how his term in office develops in the coming years will be closely watched by governments and international businesses — and by ISEAS.

OOI KEE BENG
Deputy Director, ISEAS
Founding editor of *ISEAS Perspective*

INTRODUCTION

The fourth democratic elections in post-*reformasi* Indonesia held in 2014 proved most exciting. The country showed that it had with great success institutionalized the policies and initiatives taken within the democratization process that got underway in 2008. Most notably, it is the decentralization and the implementation of direct local elections that had "given birth" to Indonesia's seventh president, Joko Widodo or Jokowi.

But by the same token, the country continues to suffer from the dysfunctionality of the institutions and the persisting socio-economic problems. As such, Indonesia's democratic progress remains a unique one, where although elections are free and civil society is vigilant in keeping government in check, many setbacks linger. Corruption is still rampant and parties continue neglecting formulating clear platforms and policies, and instead heavily on political figures to attract votes.

The collection of articles in this volume represent close-up snapshots of numerous actors and the many issues arising during the 2014 elections. Together, the contributions demonstrate various dynamics that Indonesian voters were faced with even before the real campaign had started.

To be sure, the election of Joko Widodo as governor of Jakarta in 2012 brought a profound change that clearly influenced the subsequent campaigning methods and mechanisms adopted by parties and by individual candidates.

Several articles show how political parties struggled to improve their standing in voters' eyes, amidst the various scandals and leadership problems that embroiled many of them more than a year before the elections. Non-mainstream actors such as the Islamic Defenders Front (FPI) also receive special attention with a contribution highlighting how these, despite their hostile stand against democracy, acted nevertheless, as vote brokers, through their manoeuvres.

Several shed light on the campaign dynamics at the grassroots level. The new trends and realities that parties and candidates faced that year were especially imperative to investigate — generally, parties took a much less determinant role while candidates occupied the centre stage. As was to be expected perhaps, old practices such as vote-buying became more sophisticated, and will most likely continue be an important feature in Indonesian elections in years to come.

The votes cast for the various parties also revealed new developments that Indonesia enthusiasts should take note of. These are notably the endurance of the Islam-based parties, the "failure" of the Indonesian Democratic Party – Struggle (PDI-P), and the influence on voting behaviour of charismatic leaders.

The presidential election took the form of rivalry between the old and new breeds of Indonesian leaders. On one hand, Jokowi represented the new breed that rose from the grassroots and that has few connections with the traditional elite, while his opponent, Prabowo Subianto, exemplified the old elite trying their best to retain control.

These articles also provide the assessment of the presidential campaign as one where the utilization of new and old-but-improved tactics to discredit the opponent created strong polarizing effects on voters. What transpired as a result is a divided government that now has to manage the heavy burden of high public expectations. The various multi-faceted problems and challenges that the Jokowi government faces are thoroughly discussed in these contributions.

In providing an assessment of the undercurrents and challenges that the 2014 Indonesian elections faced, this collection is crucial to an understanding of the contemporary issues that shaped the 2014 elections and that will challenge the government of President Jokowi. These dynamics suggest strongly that the future of Indonesian politics will see a strengthened role being played for individual candidates, and a continuing struggle by parties to find a role that goes beyond them being mere vehicles for candidates. Voting patterns will stay fluid and will remain vulnerable to socio-economic issues that could spell the rise and fall of leaders and parties.

1

THE GUBERNATORIAL RACE IN JAKARTA
Background and Implications

Hui Yew-Foong and Ikrar Nusa Bhakti

Of all the direct elections for local leaders (known in Indonesian as Pilkada) held in 2012, the gubernatorial race for Jakarta DKI was definitely the one to watch. As a contest for the most important posts for Indonesia's sprawling capital city with almost 7 million registered voters, the Jakarta election serves as a barometer for local elections throughout the Indonesian archipelago.

During the first round of the local election on 11 July 2012, the popular challenger, Joko "Jokowi" Widodo, led with almost 43 per cent of the votes, while the incumbent, Fauzi "Foke" Bowo, trailed with 34 per cent. As none of the candidates garnered more than 50 per cent of the votes, the two leading candidates went on to a second round run-off.

Hui Yew-Foong is an ISEAS Senior Fellow, and Ikrar Nusa Bhakti is Professor of Intermestic Affairs, Indonesian Institute of Sciences (LIPI). This article was first published on 1 November 2012 as ISEAS Perspective 2012/11.

And so, on 20 September 2012, Jakarta voters went to the polls a second time to elect their governor and deputy governor. Quick count estimates showed Jokowi winning with at least 53 per cent of the votes, and already that same day, Fauzi Bowo congratulated the new governor-elect. The Jakarta General Election Commission officially announced on 29 September that Jokowi had won 53.82 per cent of valid votes, winning the majority of the vote in all five municipalities of Jakarta. Fauzi Bowo had garnered 46.18 per cent of valid votes.

On 15 October, Joko Widodo and his running mate Basuki Tjahaja Purnama were installed as governor and deputy governor of Jakarta respectively, and became the second pair to be directly elected to two of the nation's most coveted offices.

DECENTRALIZATION AND DIRECT ELECTIONS FOR LOCAL LEADERS

In reaction to the over-centralization of state powers during the Suharto era, Indonesia embarked on a path of decentralization with legal reforms in 1999. Law No. 22/1999 and Law No. 25/1999 instituted the devolution of political authority and distribution of revenues respectively to districts and municipalities. This gave much greater power and autonomy to local leaders and local parliaments. With more at stake in terms of resources made available at the local level, political elites at that level lobbied for the proliferation of districts and municipalities. From a total of 341 in 1999, the number of districts and municipalities grew to 440 by 2004, and now stands at around 500.

When these decentralization laws were first promulgated in 2001, leaders at the provincial level (governor), the district level (district head or bupati) and municipal level (mayor) were elected by their respective local parliaments. In turn, this led to money politics where local parliamentarians gave their votes to the highest bidders, irrespective of party affiliations. To resolve such rent-seeking behaviour among the political elite and increase the legitimacy of local leaders, Law No. 32/2004 on Regional Government was introduced to institute the direct and popular election of governors, district heads and mayors. A role was retained for political parties at these elections as candidates have to be nominated by a party or coalition that had won at least 15 per cent of the votes at the most recent local parliamentary election or controlled at least 15 per cent of the seats in the local parliament. Since April 2008, this requirement was no longer necessary as Law No. 12/2008 allowed independent candidates to run for local leadership positions. All these changes in electoral laws were meant to make regional leaders directly accountable to the people they govern, and as we shall see, candidates who were more responsive and adept at communicating with the electorate stood to gain.

THE CAMPAIGN

Although Jokowi and Basuki Tjahaja Purnama, popularly known as "Ahok", were newcomers to the Jakarta political scene, they were not new to the Indonesian public eye. Jokowi, aged 51, had served as mayor of Surakarta since 2005, and was already well-known nationally for his success in running the city. He rebranded Surakarta (also known as Solo) with the motto "Solo: The Spirit of Java" and successfully applied for it to be a member of the Organization of World Heritage Cities. In a survey by the University of Indonesia and The Cyrus Network, he was found to be the most electable candidate for governor of Jakarta. Ahok, aged 46, had been bupati of East Belitung and a member of the People's Representative Council before running for deputy governor of Jakarta. Both men had also won awards for being non-corrupt. Thus, they entered the campaign scene with track records as young, effective leaders who were squeaky clean.

Fauzi "Foke" Bowo, aged 64, was very much part of the Jakarta establishment. As a Betawi or native of Jakarta, Foke had served as regional secretary of the Jakarta Government, deputy governor of Jakarta and then the first directly elected governor of Jakarta. Nachrowi "Nara" Ramli, aged 61, the deputy governor candidate, was also a Betawi and a former major general of the Indonesian Army. In contrast to the younger pair of Jokowi-Ahok, it was inevitable that Foke would seem rigid in his leadership style and distanced from the people. It also did not help that under his long watch, Jakarta's perennial problems, namely traffic jams and flooding, remained unresolved.

Targeting these longstanding problems faced by Jakartans, the Jokowi-Ahok pair promised effective policies that would bring about change in the Indonesian capital city. In particular, the younger pair seemed more willing to engage with the everyday problems of the average Jakartan, from affordable drinking water to the need to revitalize and revamp kampong and slum areas. Rather than investing in expensive campaign advertisements like the Foke camp, the Jokowi-Ahok team visited slum dwellers and gave them the sense that they were respected as human beings and not just the object of political infighting among elites.

With this approachable stance, Jokowi became a "media darling" in almost all print and electronic media. They reported positively on what he did and said and he became a media celebrity, such that even his signature checkered shirt became a sought-after item in Jakarta. The team was also able to appeal to young Jakartans through pop songs and music videos, and changing the lyrics to popular tunes to foster resonance. The slogan "Fokoke Jokowi" ("It must be Jokowi"), creatively playing on the names of the opponents, also struck a chord with those who were dissatisfied with the leadership style of Fauzi Bowo. These creative campaign messages were also disseminated through social media channels such as Facebook and Tweeter. In short, by using both traditional and new media, the Jokowi-Ahok pair was better able to connect with a broad spectrum of the Jakartan electorate, from the tech-savvy middle class to the urban poor.

THE IMPLICATIONS

First, this election showed that the personal appeal of candidates was more important than the support and endorsement of political parties in determining electability. In other words, electoral support for the respective parties did not necessarily translate into support for their official candidates. In the first round of the Jakarta election on 11 July, for example, the candidates Alex Noerdin and Nono Sampono, who were backed by major parties Golkar and the United Development Party (PPP), received only 4.67 per cent of the votes, which was less than the 4.98 per cent garnered by independent candidates Faisal Basri and Biem Benjamin. Another example was the pair Hidayat Nur Wahid and Didik Rachbini, who received only 11.72 per cent of the votes, although they were supported by the Justice and Prosperity Party (PKS) that had won 17.8 per cent of votes from Jakarta in the 2009 legislative election.

The second round result is another case in point. The Jokowi-Ahok team won although they only had the backing of the Indonesian Democratic Party Struggle (PDI-P) and the Great Indonesia Movement Party (Gerindra). On the other hand, the Foke-Nara team lost even though they had the support of all other major parties, which included the Democratic Party (PD), Golkar, PPP, PKS and the National Mandate Party (PAN). While this did not mean that political parties had become insignificant institutions, it did mean that beyond the formal political arena where parties posture and seal their alliances, political parties have little traction, especially when it came to voting behavior.

Second, in pluralistic and cosmopolitan Jakarta, the politicization of SARA (ethnic, religious, race and inter-group) issues proved to be disingenuous. Be it the highlighting of Foke and Nara's native Betawi credentials, the undermining of Ahok because he was of the Chinese minority and a Christian (read non-Muslim), or the accusation that Jokowi's mother was non-Muslim (which proved to be untrue), all these did not have a definitive impact on the polls. What seemed to be more important was the ability of the candidates to embrace a pluralistic agenda that would benefit all sectors of the electorate. This was why, other than Ahok, Chinese had been moderately successful in other gubernatorial, district and mayoral elections since direct elections were introduced in 2005.

Third, the opinion polls that politicians and political pundits depended so much upon were blatantly inaccurate. Most of the opinion polls, conducted in April by institutions such as The Cyrus Network, the Lingkaran Survei Indonesia and Indo Barometer, predicted that the Foke-Nara pair would win handsomely. Only the survey by the Institute for Economic and Social Research, Education and Information (LP3ES) put the Foke-Nara and Jokowi-Ahok teams neck to neck. This raised questions about the methodological rigor of the pollsters and the extent to which they were instruments for measuring or for swaying public opinion.

As Jakarta represents a good cross-section of Indonesia, the lessons from this recent gubernatorial election can be instructive, not only for other local elections, but also for the Presidential election due in 2014. Besides having to be sceptical about the reliability of opinion polls, presidential candidates will have to run campaigns that do not seek to capitalize on narrow communal loyalties. Instead, they will have to do more than pay lip service to pluralistic values in their visions and missions, and convince the majority of Indonesian voters that they can empathize with the average citizen and will seek to improve the lives of a broad spectrum of Indonesians. They will have to be nimble in communicating their campaign messages across both traditional and new media platforms. While those who subscribe to the latter tend to be young, middle class urbanites, constituencies of more than 50 million Facebook users and 19.5 million Tweeter users out of a population of 248 million cannot be ignored. Finally, while candidates will need the support of political parties to be nominated, such support will not be decisive at the polls. Current President Susilo Bambang Yudhoyono, whose Democratic Party was relatively small when he was first elected president in 2004, is a fitful reminder of the limits of party influence at presidential elections.

THE CHALLENGES

Jokowi and Ahok have no honeymoon period waiting for them upon assuming office. They will have to deliver results, or at least be seen to be making changes, within the first hundred days. Yet, many of the problems, including not just traffic and flooding woes, but also sanitation, healthcare, education and graft, among others, cannot be easily addressed overnight.

So far, Jokowi has been visiting villagers to understand problems at the grassroots, and opting to plough through Jakarta's infamous traffic jams instead of cruising through with motorcades. Ahok has been making unannounced visits to assess the Jakarta bureaucracy and raise accountability. The duo is also seeking to slash the city's budget and achieve savings of up to 20 per cent.

Whether any of Jakarta's problems can be resolved depends not only on the bureaucratic machinery, but also on the new leaders' ability to navigate through the political labyrinth of the capital city. As their backers, the PDI-P and Gerindra, only control 18 per cent of the seats in the Jakarta City Council, Jokowi and Ahok will have an uphill task gaining support from the Council on major decisions.

Moreover, Jakarta and its problems are much larger than Solo or East Belitung, so it is not wholly certain that Jokowi and Ahok will be able to replicate their success. It remains to be seen if the aura of hope that brought them electoral success will raise them above the quagmire of Jakarta politics. Sometimes, outsiders have the best chance of effecting change.

2

INDONESIAN PARTIES STRUGGLE FOR ELECTABILITY

Ulla Fionna

In February 2013, leaders of Indonesia's two major political parties were detained on graft suspicions. The arrests of Partai Keadilan Sejahtera's (PKS, Prosperous Justice Party) president Luthfi Hasan Ishaaq, and Partai Demokrat's (PD, Democratic Party) chairman Anas Urbaningrum have jeopardized their respective parties' electoral prospects. While Luthfi has been arrested for suspicions over special favours for certain beef importers, Anas — previously linked to other corruption cases — has allegedly received a luxury car as a bribe for fixing a government construction contract for the Hambalang sports centre project.

The arrests followed a string of other high-profile party politicians who are facing corruption charges. Indonesia's Corruption Eradication Commission (Komisi Pemberantasan Korupsi, KPK) have previously detained Andi Mallarangeng (former Sports and Youth Affairs Minister),

Ulla Fionna is Fellow at ISEAS. This article was first published on 21 March 2013 as *ISEAS Perspective* 2013/15.

and jailed Angelina Sondakh (PD's deputy secretary general) and Muhammad Nazaruddin (PD's former treasurer). Late last year, the Jakarta Corruption Court has also sentenced Wa Ode Nurhayati, a former member of the House of Representatives budgetary committee from the Partai Amanat Nasional (National Mandate Party).

For the parties involved, a lot is riding on the back of these cases. With the 2014 general election looming, parties need to figure out how to react and manage these crises. Internal conflicts and organizational problems also have to be addressed urgently. More broadly, these cases highlight the fact that the costs of party politics are high in Indonesia, and the systemic problems of party corruption needs urgent attention from the parties and the state.

PKS: THE CHALLENGE TO STAY "CLEAN" AND ISLAMIC

Born of the Jemaat Tarbiyah (Education Movement), PK (Partai Keadilan, Justice Party), the predecessor of PKS, was founded in 1998. After failing to gain a minimum of 2 per cent of the national votes in 1999, which was necessary to qualify for the next elections, the party was re-constituted as PKS in 2003 to run in the 2004 elections. As the largest Islamic party in Indonesia, which prides itself as "clean and caring", the PKS also has impressive organizational prowess, rivalled only by Partai Golkar, which has been dominant over the thirty-two years of the New Order's rule. PKS' young, committed, and technology-savvy cadres are the backbone of the frequent and wide-ranging activities at the grassroots. By itself, or in partnership with NGOs, PKS has developed a variety of activities, ranging from the regular pengajian (Quranic study group), to regular welfare and healthcare services for the poor, social services for women, to information sessions for young Muslim couples and exhibition of Islamic caricatures.

Another pillar of its success is its focused and well-managed recruitment and mobilization exercises. PKS attracts committed members because it successfully convinces them to be politically active as devout Muslims, while promising them non-discriminatory opportunities to attain political power — something that was denied them under the authoritarian

Suharto regime. Still another success factor for PKS is its ability to not rely too much on personalities. While support for Partai Kebangkitan Bangsa (National Awakening Party, PKB) is still heavily influenced by the lingering charisma of the late Abdurrahman Wahid (former president of Indonesia), and for Partai Demokrasi Indonesia Perjuangan (Indonesian Democratic Party Struggle, PDIP) by the first president Sukarno and his daughter Megawati Sukarnoputri; leadership succession in PKS has been smooth, frequent, and democratic.

The irony for this Islamic party is that it became more popular (gaining 7.34 per cent of national votes in 2004 and 7.88 per cent in 2009) after moving away from the goal of establishing an Islamic Indonesian state after its poor 1999 election results (1.36 per cent votes). The party platform has shifted quite dramatically from focusing on strongly Islamic messages, to moderation by featuring the promotion of good and clean/corruption-free governance. PKS also declared itself inclusive. One of its taglines "PKS for all" opens the party to non-Muslims, and now it boasts about a dozen parliamentary members from Christian majority electoral districts. Perhaps most surprising for its staunchly Islamic supporters was its decision to form coalitions with parties with different ideologies, including the Christian Partai Demokrasi Sejahtera (Prosperous Democratic Party, PDS), in local elections.

For the PKS, the pressure to stay popular while maintaining a clean image seems increasingly difficult to balance. Internal cracks are growing over how to carry the party forward, in particular over how to promote Islamic piety without alienating the majority nominal Muslims. Meanwhile, its clean image has been dented by accusations of graft and embezzlement from former party pioneer Jusuf Supendi. No longer with the party, he alleges that party leaders have been involved in various embezzlement and corruption cases, and has reported them to the KPK. One of the leaders that Supendi accuses is Luthfi's replacement, Anis Matta, who has also been linked to a corruption case. With a string of other allegations of corruption by party cadres, it seems that the party has been suffering hit after hit, but Luthfi's arrest is definitely the biggest blow to the party's bid for one of the top three positions in the 2014 elections.

PD: THE NEED TO STAY RELEVANT BEYOND SBY

Put simply, PD is President Susilo Bambang Yudhoyono's (SBY) party. It was first built as a vehicle for SBY who was seen as a more suitable running candidate for Megawati Sukarnoputri's (Mega) bid for presidency in 2004, than Partai Persatuan Pembangunan's (PPP, United Development Party) Hamzah Haz who once said that voting for a female president is *haram* (forbidden) in Islam. When Haz was chosen by Mega anyway, some entrepreneurs and academics decided to launch a separate political base for SBY in the form of PD. As support for direct presidential election and SBY quickly developed, so did the party. After PD was launched nationally in October 2002, the party council and branches quickly accelerated the process of getting ready for the 2004 elections.

Because of this rush, PD's organization is not as solid as PKS's. To meet the requirements that a party must have branches in two-thirds of all provinces and two-thirds of the regencies *(kabupaten)*/cities in these provinces, the party implemented no criteria for registration as party members and candidates and admitted whoever was interested and let them run for election. The party's central office had very little control over these practices. The central leadership was then dominated by businesspeople and academics with limited political experience. Consequently, the people who were interested to join were those who saw better opportunities for access to power through this new party, compared to the more established and thus saturated PDIP or Partai Golkar.

Undoubtedly, SBY himself is the star of the party. Reluctant at first, he only joined the party campaign after his high-profile resignation from Mega's cabinet, just a few weeks before the legislative election in 2004. His resignation and appeal for change attracted a lot of sympathy from the public, especially after he had been excluded from cabinet meetings by Mega. His dramatic rise in popularity became the main driver for the party, especially since it did not have strong grassroots organizations. PD became the fourth largest party — after Partai Golkar, PDI-P, and PPP — in parliament after obtaining 7.4 per cent of votes in 2004. For the presidential election, PD decided to pair SBY with Jusuf Kalla, a leading Partai Golkar figure and businessman, and won after defeating Mega in the second round.

Despite SBY's popularity and relative success in his presidency, his party has deteriorated after his inauguration. He decided to appoint only one out of nine ministerial candidates that his party proposed, displeasing party pioneers and leaders. SBY's intervention resulted in what can only be called the institutionalization of his power in the party. His brother-in-law Hadi Utomo became the party chairman (after some negotiation from SBY's wife Bu Ani); SBY himself was named chairman of Dewan Pembina (Advisory Council, the highest body in the party); Edi Baskoro Yudhoyono, SBY's son, became head of leadership training (known as Ibas, he has since been promoted to his current position as secretary general); and another of Bu Ani's brothers, Hartanto Edhi Wibowo, headed the party's department of state-owned companies.

The party then moved to recruit experienced politicians such as Andi Mallarangeng (a political scientist and media commentator) and Anas Urbaningrum (former Muslim Students' Association chairman), while senior members were sidelined to the advisory council. For the 2009 elections, SBY's popularity was further boosted by his populist programmes, such as unconditional cash handouts (Bantuan Tunai Langsung, BLT), health insurance for the poor, and fuel price reduction. Meanwhile, the election campaign by the party utilized SBY's personal charisma highlighting his achievements and policies through the media, while door-to-door campaigning was also done aggressively. The 2009 general elections saw PD becoming the most popular party in the country with more than 20 per cent of the votes. Ibas, Hartanto Edhi Wibowo, and Hadi Utomo's son Nurcahyo Anggoro were all elected to parliament, strengthening the SBY family's influence in PD. The presidential election that followed cemented SBY's popularity even further. The coalition with Partai Golkar broke up soon after the 2009 general elections, as PD grew confident that now it could have greater control of who SBY's running candidate would be. Eventually, SBY chose Boediono, a non-partisan economist and ex-Bank Indonesia governor, and they won by a landslide.

After 2009, SBY seemed to have lost his control of the party for a while, when Anas Urbaningrum won the chairman position, although SBY has strongly indicated his backing for another candidate. SBY then quickly reasserted his power by establishing the Majelis Tinggi (High Assembly, MT) — a new body tasked with all strategic decisions such as presidential candidates, coalition partners, and candidates for local elections. Anas, however, is ambitious and relentless. Although his name had been closely linked to several corruption charges (most notably, Muhammad Nazaruddin accused him as one of the people most responsible for the Hambalang case) and until early February 2013 he had endured mounting pressure to resign from other party officials, he kept his position in the hope of making a bid for the 2014 presidential candidacy. Intra-party conflict was so severe that SBY had to step in and intervene, yet again.

WINNERS AND LOSERS IN THE MAKING

Both PKS's and PD's electability suffered severely because of the arrest of their leaders. The latest poll placed PKS seventh among the ten competing parties, while PD is fourth — a serious decline compared to its big win in 2009. Although PKS leaders have played down these statistics, they did admit that Luthfi's arrest has forced their popularity to take a nose dive. Similarly for PD, polls suggest that it is now perceived as the most corrupt party in the country. Alarmingly for PD, as much as 51 per cent of respondents identified the party as the most corrupt, while Partai Golkar came second with only 5.4 per cent. This poll was conducted before Anas' arrest, so party officials are bracing themselves for even worse results in the near future.

Looking further into the aftermath of these arrests, how the parties have reacted could raise concerns. Anis Matta claimed that the arrest was a conspiracy against the party. Although other party leaders then tried to soften this accusation by focusing on visitation programmes from national leaders to visit grassroots branches for consolidation and calling for "national repentance" to deal with the crisis, the defiance demonstrates the party's refusal to respect the law. Things are no different in PD, with Anas commenting that his arrest "is only the first page" — fuelling speculations that he will reveal other cases of corruption involving other important national figures. These reactions and comments indicate the plausible gravity of these scandals, and the fierce party competition before the elections. It also points to Anas' resentment towards the lack of support from SBY, and created a more intense rift between his supporters and SBY's in the party. Just days before Anas' arrest, he was ordered by the

Majelis Tinggi (headed by SBY) to focus on his legal problems, while Ibas Yudhoyono stepped down from parliament to assist with PD's internal consolidation. However, Anas, who is under house arrest, has been visited by numerous national politicians and figures, indicating his popularity and the support he has garnered. So now, although Ibas has been named as a strong candidate to replace Anas, SBY may want to be more tactful in managing his family's interest in the party.

PD serves as a strong warning against relying too much on leadership charisma and the failure to establish solid party machinery. Long before SBY served both his terms, the party should have established a more solid platform and machinery that could carry it past the convenience of having a charismatic leading figure. Unfortunately for PD, SBY does not seem to realize this. His grip on the party is now even stronger after Anas is ousted. Unless SBY decentralizes authority and limits his family's influence, the party's image and future will be compromised even further.

From the organizational point of view, the case of PKS paints a depressing picture. A showcase of solid organizational capacity, the party still suffers from disunity and the challenge of maintaining a solid Islamic outlook that is non-discriminative. The party needs to settle internal differences once and for all, and then decide which direction it is going to take, in order to retain popularity and votes.

The trend of internal conflict (although not corruption-related) is also observed in the case of Partai Nasdem (National Democratic Party). Backed by some of the most prominent figures in Indonesian media and academics, Partai Nasdem seems to be the one to watch for the next election, which will be its first. However, days after the Election Commission (KPU) announced the allocated numbers for the ten contesting parties, the party was deserted by one of its founders, media mogul Hary Tanoesoedibjo. Claiming that his wish to see the younger generation lead the party has been disapproved by national council chairman Surya Paloh, who prefers the more mature/experienced politicians, Hary resigned and triggered a mass exodus of his followers. His media empire and financial strength would certainly have been an asset for the party campaign and, needless to say, the party's electoral chances are worse off as a result. Although the cause behind the unravelling of Partai Nasdem seems different from what is happening in PKS and PD, the case confirms the intense pressure to find the best electoral strategy.

The rise and fall of political parties in a democracy is normal, and a consolidated democracy will select which parties will survive eventually. From this point of view the scandals can be seen as positive as they point to the corrupt practices of parties and indeed the depth of party corruption in Indonesia. The parties seen as the least corrupt and can function the best should survive better, and parties are taking note of this. However, the high cost of establishing a new party and indeed party politics in general, have led parties to corrupt practices. For instance, a new party has to have branches in at least two-thirds of all provinces and two-thirds of all regencies in all these provinces — leading to high startup costs. The reduction in state party financing, and the frequency of direct local elections have produced corrupt parties with illegal fund-raising activities, and party functionaries who siphon monies off from state budgets for the parties and to enrich themselves. Fierce competition has also forced parties to engage political consultants, which has driven the cost even further. The call for greater transparency for their fund-generating activities may discourage illegal practices. However, whether such a suggestion will be realized in a bill is doubtful. It is quite unlikely that the legislature, made up of party politicians, will vote for a regulation that may complicate their own daily operations. So it is up to the consolidated yet new democracy to find solutions to party finance problems, and to let the voters decide the kind of parties that will survive.

Selected References

Hamayotsu, Kikue. "Beyond faith and identity: mobilizing Islamic youth in a democratic Indonesia", *The Pacific Review* 24, no. 2 (2011): 225–47.

Honna, Jun. "Inside the Democrat Party: power, politics and conflict in Indonesia's Presidential Party". *South East Asia Research* 20, no. 4 (2012): 473–89.

Mietzner, Marcus. "Party Financing in Post-Soeharto Indonesia: Between State Subsidies and Political Corruption". *Contemporary Southeast Asia* 29, no. 2 (2007): 238–63.

Taniwidjaja, Sunny. "PKS in post-Reformasi Indonesia: Catching the catch-all and moderation wave". *South East Asia Research* 20, no. 4 (2012): 533–49.

3

WHO WILL BE INDONESIAN PRESIDENT IN 2014?

Max Lane

INTRODUCTION

The usual path to become a presidential candidate in Indonesia is to be nominated by a political party or combination of parties that have either won 20 per cent of the national vote in the parliamentary elections or control 25 per cent of the seats in the House of Representatives (DPR). Some parties already have made clear choices: Golkar (Party of Functional Groups) has nominated ex-Suharto loyalist and tycoon Aburizal Bakrie (although former vice-president Yusuf Kalla still lurks in the wings as a possible challenger); Gerindra (Great Indonesia Movement Party) decided on ex-Suharto general and semi-tycoon Prabowo Subianto; Hanura

Max Lane was invited by ISEAS to give a public seminar on 5 July 2013 on the subject on which this article is based. Dr Lane is a Lecturer in Southeast Asian politics and history at Victoria University and an Honorary Associate in Indonesian Studies at the University of Sydney. This article was first published on 18 July 2013 as *ISEAS Perspective* 2013/46.

(People's Conscience Party) nominated ex-Suharto general Wiranto; and Nasdem (National Democrat Party) chose ex-Suharto loyalist and tycoon Surya Paloh. The lead party in the ruling coalition, the Democrat Party (PD), has not yet decided on its candidate although it has now moved to bring former General Pramono Edhie Wibowo, into the leadership.

The party that does have a chance of winning 20 per cent of the popular vote is the PDI-P (Indonesian Democratic Party–Struggle), but it has also yet to determine a candidate. In the past, it has nominated Megawati Sukarnoputri. There is also a possibility that the PDI-P could nominate the current governor of Jakarta, the popular Joko Widodo.

However, an analysis of candidate choice must take into consideration the steady alienation of the majority of the population from existing political processes and actors.

"REFORMASI" AND POLITICAL ALIENATION

During the 1990s, peaking in 1997–98, a movement developed demanding *reformasi* whose main demands were the departure of President Suharto, withdrawal of the army from politics, liberalization of repressive political laws, and the ending of KKN (Corruption, Collusion and Nepotism). The sentiment of this movement reflected a desire for a shift away from an authoritarian system which defended a self-seeking elite to a political system where the *rakyat* (the common people) would be listened to and its interests promoted over that of the elite. It was a movement strong enough to dislodge an authoritarian leader defended by the military.

By 1999, elections were held under a liberal election law. The movement had emerged after almost thirty years of deep authoritarian rule built upon a period of extreme repression and political engineering from 1965 to 1971. It was thus unable to build on any pre-existing organizations, such as trade unions, political groups or popular associations. Perhaps even more important to note is that, by the 1990s, all political traditions that may have provided an ideological basis for opposition — such as liberalism, liberal democracy, social democracy, socialism, and communism — had been eliminated.

This meant that the movement was unable to create a solid infrastructure of its own. Nor did it have time to develop authoritative leadership. During

1997 and 1998, political figures who had been either closely associated with the New Order[1] or who had been acquiescing marginal participants, such as Megawati Sukarnoputri (a silent M.P. under Suharto) and Amien Rais, a member of the Suharto-headed Indonesian Islam Intellectuals Association (ICMI), were able to piggy-back on the movement to win a national profile.

The consequence has been that the *reformasi* movement did not develop the structure to contest power with the various components of the New Order. Suharto, his family and his closest political allies had their power terminated, but all the other components of the system he established still dominated the scene. The movement's *temporary* character meant that no section of society that was a part of the movement, or sympathetic to it, was able to organize itself sufficiently to become a serious political institution.

The collapse of authoritarian rule also quickly revealed the structure of the broader ruling class that had developed during the New Order period. It comprised a small number of ex-crony tycoons, a few scores of middle level tycoons based in Jakarta, Surabaya, Makassar and Medan, and thousands of smaller capitalists operating at the *kabupaten* (district) or provincial level, sometimes connected to the civil service via family ties. The tycoons quickly entered into competition with each other. Two even established their own political parties.[2] Their party from the New Order era, Golkar, weakened rapidly. With no united national tycoon bloc (and no *reformasi* bloc either), the elite at the local level, on all islands, including Java, quickly supported calls for decentralization of budgetary power.

Almost ten years of high prices in commodities such as coal and palm oil, had financed widespread corruption among these elites, and facilitated a rapid expansion of a middle class with high levels of disposable income. This class now makes up perhaps 10 per cent of the population. However, the vast majority of the working population lives on less than $5 per day, many on less than $2. According to the Indonesian Bureau of Statistics, both agricultural and non-agricultural workers earning less than $200 per month have experienced a decline in real wages over recent years. The growth of the middle class is something the government has proclaimed as a measure of its success. However, the visibility of its high levels of consumption, haughty behavior and the high profile of corruption cases have exacerbated the sense of alienation among the remaining 90 per cent.

POLITICAL MANIFESTATION OF ALIENATION

Voter participation for the 1999 elections was high at almost 90 per cent. Since then, for both national and local elections, voter abstention (known as *golput*) has steadily increased. The term *golput* emerged in the 1990s when students protested against Suharto with a call to boycott the elections. The *golput* numbers, including those who do not register as voters and those who have registered but do not vote or intentionally spoil their votes, now regularly reach between 40–50 per cent. Even in the 2012 elections, the *golput* figure was almost 40 per cent for the governor of Jakarta where "popular" former Mayor of Solo, Joko Widodo, stood. This reflects the alienation of the masses from the system and is reinforced by declining support for all of the political parties. Only the very new parties increased their vote to below 5 per cent from their zero starting point. In 1999, PDI-P scored 33.74 per cent of the vote. By 2009, this had fallen to 14.03 per cent. Most polls now put the PDI-P at a higher figure of around 20 per cent, but this is still way below its 1999 support rate. GOLKAR has gone from 22.4 per cent in 1999 to 14.45 per cent in 2009 and polls now put it around 12 per cent.

President Susilo Bambang Yudhoyono's Democrat Party (PD) scored 7.45 per cent in 2004, which increased to 20.85 per cent in 2009, based on the popularity of its leader. However, following a series of corruption scandals among its leadership, the PD is now scoring less than 10 per cent. Another newer party, the Prosperous Justice Party (PKS), scored 7.34 per cent in 2004 and about the same (7.88 per cent) in 2009. However, it has also been hit by high level corruption and sex scandals and is facing declining approval ratings.

To put it bluntly, Indonesia is now a country where the most popular party in the polls, the PDI-P, is scoring only 20 per cent and all other parties are scoring 12 per cent and below.

JOKO WIDODO AND THE CONTRADICTIONS OF ALIENATION

Direct elections were introduced for the position of President and Vice-President at the national level in 2004. Previously these were elected by the Peoples' Consultative Assembly (MPR). Additionally, reflecting the influence of the newly liberated (from centralized crony rule) local bourgeoisie, direct elections were introduced for the positions of governor, *bupati* and mayor. These are in addition to the five yearly elections for national, provincial and local parliaments.

This shift to extensive electoral activity is a break with the political culture of the previous decades. Rather than the charisma or "awe" of power and authority associated with a dominant state official (*pejabat*), a "revolutionary" new principle is introduced: a politician must be popular, whatever the basis for that popularity. The first response of parties was to recruit television or religious celebrities, although this does not seem to have stopped the decline in their support.

There are now two modes of political campaigning. One is based on an appeal to the charisma of power and authority, *pejabatism*, a mode inherited from the previous era. The other is based on the deliberate rejection of this mode. The most well-known representative of the new mode is the current governor of Jakarta, Joko Widodo. As the PDI-P candidate for mayor of Solo in 2004, he won with the usual 30 plus per cent. But in 2009 he won the election with 91 per cent of the votes. In Jakarta, in 2012, he won a very high 43 per cent in the first round against five other candidates, including the incumbent Fauzi Bowo, who was backed by President Yudhoyono and his coalition. Bowo scored 33 per cent. Voter abstention was however still almost 40 per cent.

Unlike all other officials, Joko Widodo had no pictures of himself placed anywhere in public. He disarmed the village militia and negotiated directly with squatters and street peddlers. He seldom wore uniforms and dressed casually (often in a checked short-sleeve shirt, for example). He met with demonstrators, rather than dispersed them. He was appealing to the *reformasi* sentiment for the *rakyat* (the common people) to be listened to. He also implemented in Solo what can be described as social safety net policies, somewhat increasing expenditure on health, education and small scale *kampung* (village) infrastructural development. He was able to do this during his eight-year tenure by reallocating some budget items, but, more crucially, as a result of receiving large increases of revenue from the national government. His budget in his final year was 400 per cent above what it was when he first became mayor. This 400 per cent increase reflects a 400 per cent increase in national government revenue between 2004 and 2013 (mainly a result of high coal prices).

DYNAMICS OF THE 2014 ELECTIONS

In this situation, it is increasingly possible that the coming elections will take the form of a contest between these two modes of politics and the interests they are connected with at this stage.

The PDI-P's "revival" from 14 per cent in 2009 to 20 per cent in current polling is a result of it being seen as being separate from the establishment and having some of the populist gloss of figures like Widodo rubbing off onto it. Other figures like Tri Rismaharini, mayor of Surabaya, and PDI-P Members of Parliament like Rieke Pitaloka and Ribka Tjiptaning, who exhibit a maverick social democratic style, have also helped. Pitaloka, especially, played a leading role in a campaign for a Social Insurance Law, which was passed in Parliament in 2011. Megawati has also used this period to talk about the ideological reorientation of the party and regeneration of cadres.

Megawati may try to adopt some of Widodo's methods as a presidential candidate, take Widodo on board as a Vice-Presidential candidate, or she could decline to be nominated and support Widodo as presidential candidate instead. On 28 May, Megawati's daughter, Puan Maharani, chairperson of the PDI-P Central Leadership Council, indicated that the party had certainly not ruled out Widodo being its nominee, while urging him to maintain a focus on his current task as Jakarta governor.[3] Widodo in the meantime has changed his earlier public assurance that he would stay governor in Jakarta; and now suggests that whether or not he runs for President is "up to Ibu Mega."[4]

On 27 June, the Indonesian Academy of Sciences (LIPI) issued survey results naming Widodo as the most electable presidential candidate with a 22 per cent support rate. The other candidates rated as follows: Prabowo Subianto at 14.2 per cent, Aburizal Bakrie at 9.4 per cent; Megawati Soekarnoputri at 9.3 per cent, Jusuf Kalla at 4.2 per cent, and a few others scoring below 2 per cent.

An early decision to nominate Widodo may be seen as too sudden an abandonment of his Jakarta responsibilities. This could backfire if he is seen as an ambitious *pejabat*. The shift to a new basis for popularity requires having policy achievements. Therefore, Widodo will need to be seen as making progress before the PDI-P announces a decision. Moreover, his honeymoon period as governor may already be over, since he has angered the trade union movement by approving hundreds of companies' requests to postpone the implementation of the recently instituted minimum wage.[5] The PDI-P may also be postponing its decision till it becomes clearer who its main challenger may be.

Meanwhile, Yudhoyono's PD has been in crisis mode following a series of corruption scandals at its top levels. While Yudhoyono's son and wife have been touted as possible presidential candidates, it seems that such a vulgar dynastical path may be difficult to follow through in the light of the scandals. Without other candidates of stature, former Chief of Staff of the Army (2011–13), Pramono Edhie Wibowo, who was made a member of the Board of Governors in June, is a possible candidate, although nominating him would have to be a very late move that by no means guarantees success.

Another former general who has declared his candidacy is Prabowo Subianto of Gerindra. Subianto is more controversial and more strongly associated with the New Order's reputation for repression. He played an active role in 1997 and 1998 in trying to preserve the Suharto government in the face of popular opposition, even to the extent of organizing the kidnapping of student activists. He was eventually dismissed from the Army for these actions. Subianto's difficulty is that Gerindra is also unlikely, based on present indications, to win more than 20 per cent of the popular vote. In 2009, Gerindra only received 4.4 per cent of the popular vote, while recent polls suggest that its support rating is at 11 per cent. Subianto's profile is based more on a perceived comparison, in some segments of the electorate, with Yudhoyono, where the latter is seen to be without combat experience and to be indecisive, while the former is seen as a decisive combat officer. However, this niche will not come into play since Subianto will not be facing Yudhoyono in the 2014 election.

In the 2004 election, Subianto stood as Vice-President in a Megawati-Subianto team. Could this happen again? Gerindra's parliamentary record has seen it align more frequently with the ruling coalition than with the PDI-P. Even in June this year when Gerindra voted against fuel price increases, along with the PDI-P (and Hanura and PKS), it did so in a last minute switch. Gerindra and Prabowo used rhetoric that is similar to those of the PDI-P on the "peoples' economics" and so on, but it has also spoken out *against* wage rises and labour demonstrations[6] while the PDI-P has associated itself *with* such demands.

More fundamentally, Subianto and Gerindra clearly are of the old mode of politcs. This is reflected in Gerindra's preference for ending local elections and its support for retaining prison sentences for "insulting" public officials.[7]

Other potential candidates are Golkar's Bakrie or Kalla and Nasdem's Surya Palo. Their status as tycoons will make them weak candidates against Widodo or a Megawati-Widodo pairing, although Kalla's status as a tycoon is less emphasized. All these parties will not differ greatly in voter support, which will be weaker than 20 per cent. Which ones will have the upper hand in negotiations is difficult to predict at this stage.

LIMITATIONS OF THE NEW DYNAMICS

The "new politics", however, has a shallowness to it, even if the social contradictions that have facilitated its emergence are real. It will also be very difficult to retreat from elections (although Subianto has raised the idea of ending direct elections at the local level). Nor will the context change, namely, high levels of corruption among a self-interested elite, a growing middle class with ostentatious levels of corruption and declining real wages and conditions of 180 million rural and urban workers.

Widodo's and the PDI-P's "populism", if it can be called that, most likely is a transitional phenomenon. Its emergence and rise heighten expectations and legitimize appeals to the common people, the mass of the poor. Widodo's appeal to the common people is explicitly aimed at encouraging them not to organize or mobilize. Widodo has not tried to build or strengthen the PDI-P or any other organization as a vehicle for organization and mobilization. His approach is primarily electoral, aimed at mobilizing votes rather than movements.

The ultimate vote orientation in Widodo's politics can give it a very opportunistic character. This was reflected in the PDI-P's and Widodo's alliance with Gerindra and Subianto for the Jakarta gubernatorial election, with Widodo running with a Gerindra member as deputy governor.

A clear possibility is that the existence of rival modes of politics will be reflected in a contest between the PDI-P, with Widodo involved, even as presidential candidate, and a coalition that will select a candidate representing firmness and authority, such as former military figures (Wibowo or Subianto, for example). However, the shallowness and opportunism of the "populist" alternative mean that it is not impossible to envisage an alliance composing both modes of politics, such as another PDI-P-Gerindra coalition in the form of a Megawati-Subianto or Widodo-Subianto candidature. Gerindra, however, recently stated that it would support Widodo for the presidential election in 2019 but not in 2014.[8] Under this cloud of uncertainty, perhaps the most certain thing is that the likely "winner" of the election will be *golput*. The political gap between *reformasi* sentiment/aspirations and what the system is offering will not be bridged by 2014.

Notes

1. The "New Order" was coined by the second Indonesian President Suharto as he came to power in 1966, to contrast his rule from that of his predecessor, Sukarno.

2. They include Surya Paloh, who formed Nasdem, and Prabowo Subianto, who formed Gerindra. Both had previously vied for leadership of Golkar. Media tycoon Hary Tanoesoedibjo, who had been with Nasdem, has now switched to Wiranto's Hanura party, which has announced a Wiranto-Hary Tanoe pairing for the President-Vice-President candidacy.

3. <http://us.politik.news.viva.co.id/news/read/416449-puan--pdip-pertimbangkan-usung-jokowi-jadi-capres> (28 May 2013).

4. <http://www.merdeka.com/politik/jokowi-soal-capres-tanya-ibu-mega.html>.

5. <http://megapolitan.kompas.com/read/2013/04/22/16054279/Somasi.Tak.Ditanggapi.Buruh.Gugat.Jokowi> (April 2013).

6. <http://www.asia-pacific-solidarity.net/southeastasia/indonesia/indoleft/2012/detik_prabowocriticiseswork-ers_181212.htm>.

7. <http://www.thejakartapost.com/news/2013/03/27/gerindra-wants-president-s-critics-jailed.html>.

8. <http://nasional.kompas.com/read/2013/05/19/2247518> (19 May 2013).

4

INDONESIAN PRESIDENTIAL ELECTION FORCING REJUVENATION OF PARTIES

Ulla Fionna

INTRODUCTION

With Indonesian elections about six months away, speculation is mounting about who will be running to become the next directly-elected president. Which *sosok* (figure) will be chosen to represent the respective parties will be a crucial matter and will strongly influence how the presidential campaign is managed. Parties need therefore to choose their potential candidate very strategically.

Be that as it may, many parties are unable to escape the grip of traditional party authority or dynastic politics. These are either forced to nominate "old faces" or run the risk of not fielding a credible internal candidate. The nomination of veterans such as Aburizal Bakrie (Partai Golkar/Golkar Party), Wiranto (Partai Hati Nurani Rakyat/People's

Ulla Fionna is Fellow at ISEAS. This article was first published on 18 November 2013 as *ISEAS Perspective* 2013/60.

Conscience Party), Prabowo Subianto (Partai Gerakan Indonesia Raya/ Great Indonesia Movement Party), and the lack of suitable candidates in Partai Demokrat (PD, Democratic Party) are evidence of this succession problem. Partai Demokrasi Indonesia–Perjuangan (PDI-P, Indonesian Democratic Party Struggle), on the other hand, has developed an alternative system of candidate selection through nurturing local candidates for national leadership.

By all accounts, the battle among the parties to present the most credible presidential candidate will be uncompromising. This essay analyses the strategies of two major parties in their bid to win the popular vote.

PD'S NATIONAL CONVENTION: THE SEARCH FOR SUCCESSOR

PD is by most accounts a success story. It was built as a political vehicle as late as in 2001 to carry Susilo Bambang Yudhoyono in his bid for presidency in the 2004 elections. The party has since then been riding on his success. After a rushed set-up, Yudhoyono's meteoric rise in popularity propelled PD to become the fourth largest political party in 2004 with 7.04 per cent of the votes, behind Partai Golkar (Golkar Party), PDI-P, and Partai Persatuan Pembangunan (PPP, United Development Party). The party's strength grew further in the 2009 elections. It secured more than 20 per cent of the votes and tripled its number of seats in the legislature from 55 seats in 2004 to 148 seats.

Arguably, Yudhoyono's popularity single-handedly carried his party in the last two elections. However, relying too much on one *sosok* has its consequences. Since the landslide victory in 2009, it appears that Yudhoyono has been losing his grip over the party with intensifying rivalry developing between his supporters and loyalists of Anas Urbaningrum who became party chairman the following year. Yudhoyono countered Anas' victory by establishing the Majelis Tinggi (High Assembly, MT) and tasked it with all strategic decisions. Anas' power diminished after he allegedly took a bribe in relation to the construction of the Hambalang sports centre project.[1] Although he resigned, the party's public standing took a heavy beating from corruption scandals which also included criminal charges levied on other PD officials: Muhammad Nazaruddin (former party treasurer),

Angelina Sondakh (former secretary general), and Andi Mallarangeng (former Sports and Youth Minister).

As Yudhoyono's second term comes to an end, PD is searching for a successor. The President has consulted a few of his trusted party leaders, and has arranged a party convention for nominees who have been shortlisted to become its presidential candidate. Modified from the American party convention, PD has made a list of internal candidates, and another for external candidates. Although technically anyone can register to be included as candidate, it is really the Komite Konvensi Pencalonan Presiden (Committee of Convention for Presidential Candidates) — headed by Yudhoyono and made up of public and party officials — who eventually decides who goes onto the list. The individuals who were considered included former vice-president Jusuf Kalla of Golkar Party, and former Constitutional Court chief justice Mahfud MD. However both of them have declined PD's invitation to join the convention.

Yudhoyono is said to be uneasy about the possible inclusion of his wife, Kristiani Herawati or "Bu Ani" as she is affectionately called, and her brother's name in the list. Although his wife's name was eventually dropped, her brother — former army general Pramono Edhi Wibowo (whose familial connection made him a sort of heir apparent) — is now one of the strongest candidates from within the party. The other ten candidates who have been invited to join the convention, who have been interviewed, and who have made it to the final list are: Supreme Audit Agency (BPK) member Ali Masykur Musa; Paramadina University' Rector Anies Baswedan; State-Owned Enterprises Minister Dahlan Iskan; Indonesian Ambassador to the US Dino Patti Djalal; former Indonesian Military (TNI) commander Endriartono Sutarto; Trade Minister Gita Wirjawan; Regional Representatives Council (DPD) Speaker Irman Gusman; House Commission I member Hayono Isman; speaker of the People's Representative Council and PD official Marzuki Alie; and North Sulawesi Governor Sinyo Harry Sarundajang.

These candidates have started their political campaigns. They will subsequently participate in a series of public debates scheduled from January to May 2014 which will focus on their mission, vision, programme, and problem-solving ideas. And unlike the U.S. system where voters directly cast their ballots, the committee will contract a reputable and independent pollster to poll and decide on the final candidate. The party has voiced its confidence on this new process and has positioned it as a breakthrough in giving equal chance to the candidates in their campaign effort. It has also sought to assure voters that the final decision will be transparent with the survey being conducted by credible polling agencies. In any case, it is in PD's interest to pick the best candidate to pit against candidates from the other parties.

A CRYPTIC ENDORSEMENT OF JOKOWI?

As a successor to Sukarno's Partai Nasional Indonesia (PNI, Indonesian Nationalist Party) and Partai Demokrasi Indonesia (PDI, Indonesian Democratic Party), PDI-P has always been a major party in Indonesia. Headed by Megawati Sukarnoputri — the country's former president (2001–04) and Sukarno's daughter — PDI-P has grown to become a strong opposition party since 2004. While other major parties such as Partai Keadilan Sejahtera (PKS, Prosperous Justice Party) and PD have been struggling to boost their electability, PDI-P has managed to stay ahead in the polls. A survey done in late August by Kompas put PDI-P in the lead with 23.6 per cent; and Forum Akademisi Informasi Teknologi even gave PDI-P 34 per cent — surpassing the threshold to nominate presidential candidate without coalition.[2]

Legal cases being expedited against members of other parties and the tendency for a candidate's popularity to affect voting behaviour have certainly worked in favour of PDI-P who counts Indonesia's man-of-the-moment among their ranks — Jakarta governor Joko Widodo, known locally as Jokowi. Garnering an average of more than 20 per cent in most polls since early 2013, his candidacy has been the subject of much speculation.

Jokowi certainly fits the profile of a candidate that PDI-P would endorse and put forth for election: he is a Javanese and already possessed local leadership experience as mayor of Solo before becoming Jakarta's number one man. While the party has been delaying the announcement of an official candidate for the presidential race, there are strong signs that Jokowi is tipped for the position. For instance, he was given the symbolic role of reciting *Dedication of Life* — a speech which was first written and read by Sukarno in 1966 when he was in office — at the party's National

Working Meeting in September at which electoral strategies and national leadership issues were discussed. He has also been deployed by Megawati to draw support for other PDI-P candidates in other localities, and he usually becomes the primary attraction in these events.

Paving the way for a regeneration of party leadership, Megawati herself has reiterated that she would not compete in the race. Referring to her previous losses, including a crushing defeat in the 2009 poll when she captured about a quarter of the votes compared to more than 60 per cent for Yudhoyono, she identified herself as a "grandmother who has lost three times before" and does not stand a chance.[3]

PDI-P's internal polls in its branches in July have also indicated strong support of 60 per cent for Jokowi compared to 30 per cent for Megawati. However, conservative members within the party prefer Megawati to run again, while other factions have suggested that Jokowi should pair up with Puan Maharani (Megawati's daughter and the Chair of PDI-P Fraction in People's Representative Council) or with a candidate from other party/-ies.[4]

Whichever the scenario PDI-P will eventually choose, the party has set a high vote target of 27.02 per cent for the 2014 elections. And the voters' demand seems already clear: Jokowi for president. Opinion polls conducted by Forum Akademisi Informasi Teknologi indicated that — if he runs — PDI-P will not only emerge the big winner, but there will also be less non-voters (*golongan putih/golput*). Around 25.5 per cent of voters have indicated that they will not vote if Jokowi does not run, while the figure drops to 19.7 per cent if Jokowi does.[5] In any case, Jokowi's popularity means that Megawati is likely to give way to him.

ESCAPING THE DYNASTIC TRAP

Direct local elections and the current system of presidential appointment have meant that parties have to engage in strategic selection of their presidential candidates. However, credible and/or popular candidates are hard to find. The comparative analysis of PD and PDI-P demonstrates this dilemma: while PD's heavy reliance on the pulling power of Yudhoyono has limited its capacity to develop internal cadres, PDI-P — although similarly also reliant on Megawati's leadership — has managed to nurture local candidates for national leadership.

Yudhoyono has continued to carve out his personal influence by accumulating and exerting power as the chairman of PD's Dewan Pembina (Advisory Council). In addition, his wife, son, nephew, and brothers-in-law occupy various leadership positions within the party. PD's difficulty in developing internal cadres is compounded by the fact that its strongest presidential candidate is also Yudhoyono's brother-in-law, retired military general Pramono Edhi Wibowo. Pramono was provided with a recruitment short-cut, by virtue of his appointment as a member of the Advisory Council merely four days after joining the party, and then named as one of the eleven candidates for the party convention. These developments point towards PD's desperation especially as the popularity rate of all its eleven candidates is negligible, according to polls. To make matters worse, Pramono's candidacy also serves as further evidence of the dynastic and colluded politics in the party. It is also noteworthy that PD invited Jokowi, perhaps another sign of its desperation, as potential candidate for the national convention — an invitation that the PDI-P loyalist declined.

In contrast, although Megawati also has the last say in PDI-P, the party has successfully housed a number of candidates that are attracting a lot of voter attention. And although staying in opposition has given the party limited access to state budgets, this also means that it has had fewer opportunities to engage in corrupt practices which have resulted in a much better and cleaner image for the party.[6] At the same time, Megawati demonstrates a much more open mind on candidacy in contrast to Yudhoyono. Although her daughter Puan Maharani is also a strong party candidate for presidency, Megawati has been keeping an eye on other rising candidates. Puan, who chairs the PDI-P faction at the House of Representatives, credits the rise of Jokowi as evidence of party regeneration. She claims that regeneration was initiated ten years ago within the party, with the party monitoring local leaders for promotion to higher levels in the party's administration.[7] While commentaries suggest that grassroots recruitment in PDI-P may not be a defining feature of the party's succession strategy,[8] Puan's claim supports evidence of a successful monitoring mechanism that serves to identify promising local leaders.

Aside from Jokowi, PDI-P is building up promising political careers for several other local leaders in Indonesia, such as Ganjar Pranowo (Central

Java governor) and Rustriningsih (former deputy governor of Central Java). The party has even laid claims to being behind the rise of Surabaya mayor Tri Rismaharini. The new breed of PDI-P cadres demonstrates that Indonesian parties are capable of nurturing their own file-and-rank members without relying on dynastic politics. They have also boosted party reputation by projecting a cleaner image, which is a strong draw for voters who are fed up with the numerous corruption scandals emanating from the country's political elite.

If PDI-P manages to keep this momentum up and achieve a majority win in the 2014 general elections, the party will have a strong position entering the presidential elections. However, if elected into government, they will need to live up to voters' expectations of cleanliness — which is a different matter altogether.

Notes

1. Anas is presently under house arrest and is yet to be tried. He has managed to declare a new mass organization called Indonesian Movement Association/ Perhimpunan Pergerakan Indonesia.
2. Bestian Nainggolan, "Survei Kompas: Sosok Selamatkan Partai", *Kompas*, 27 August 2013; Elvan Dany Sutrisno, "Jika Capreskan Jokowi, PDI-P Tak Perlu Koalisi", detiknews, 27 August 2013. The threshold to nominate presidential candidate without coalition is 20 per cent of seats in the People's Representative Council (DPR, Dewan Permusyawaratan Rakyat), or 25 per cent of total votes.
3. Seto Wardhana, "Restu Mantan untuk Sang Calon", *Tempo*, 11 August 2013, p. 35.
4. "Di Panggung Punggung Partai Banteng", *Tempo*, 15 September 2013, pp. 37–38.
5. Elvan Dany Sutrisno, "Jika Capreskan Jokowi, PDI-P Tak Perlu Koalisi", detiknews, 27 August 2013.
6. This is the case particularly compared to PD, which after the arrests of multiple cadres, is now perceived by as much as 51 per cent of survey respondents as the most corrupt.
7. Andi Muttya Keteng, "Jokowi Nyapres, Regenerasi PDI-P Sukses?", Liputan 6.com, 6 September 2013.
8. For example Ulla Fionna, *The Institutionalisation of Political Parties in Post-authoritarian Indonesia: From the Grassroots Up* (Amsterdam: University of Amsterdam Press, 2013).

5

RESISTING DEMOCRACY
Front Pembela Islam and Indonesia's 2014 Elections

Ian Wilson

INTRODUCTION

"Democracy is more dangerous than pig's meat!" declared Habib Rizieq Shihab, leader of the Front Pembela Islam (FPI; Defenders of Islam Front) during a speech at a local branch in West Java in April 2013.[1] According to Rizieq, embracing democracy was tantamount to abandoning fundamentals of the Islamic faith, posing a far greater threat to the spiritual integrity of the *ummah* than the consumption of forbidden substances such as pork. "If we consume pig", he stated, "we are polluted, but can still be returned to a state of purity if we cleanse ourselves seven times. If we eat it we've sinned, however we haven't become an infidel."

Ian Wilson is Research Fellow at the Asia Research Centre and Lecturer in Politics, Development and Security Studies at the School of Management and Governance, Murdoch University, Western Australia. This article was first published on 24 February 2014 as *ISEAS Perspective* 2014/10.

Democracy, however, he argued, marks an irredeemable point of no return. "If democracy is fully embraced by Muslims, and the laws of Allah in turn ignored, then they become apostates (*murtad*). Democracy can transform us into infidels".

Established in 1998, and initially subsidized by the military and police as part of a street-level militia mobilized against the student-led reform movement, the FPI has now for over fifteen years expressed "alarm" and outrage at liberal democracy, representing it as a threat to Islamic practice and belief. Many in Indonesia consider it the latest manifestation of political thuggery, albeit wearing religious robes rather than the camouflage fatigues of former regime henchmen such as the *Pemuda Pancasila*, but with far greater autonomy from its patrons; itself a product of the greater freedom of organization available in the post-New Order period. Its mission statement, the Quranic edict of *amar makruf nahi mungkar* (to command the good and forbid the bad), is framed as a necessary defensive response to the excesses unleashed by Indonesia's post-authoritarian transition. As one FPI leader expressed it, "democratic reform opened the door for change, the problem however is that just about anyone or anything has been able to walk through that door...pornographers, homosexuals, apostates, all manner of heresy and deviancy". The door of democratic reform, in their opinion, needs to be closed shut.

Despite its unambiguous rejection of electoral democracy as being antithetical to Islam, and as a virtual "pathway to hell", hardliners and conservatives such as the FPI have nonetheless proved adept in playing a particular kind of politics shaped by the broader framework of Indonesia's decentralized electoral system. The FPI has carved out a niche for itself in the political landscape by intentionally prising open social tensions and instigating moral panics through which it has sought to situate itself as a broker; as a kind of morality racketeer. Some of its successes include pressuring the state to legalize the persecution of religious minorities (in particular followers of the Ahmadiyah sect); politicizing the previously uncontentious issue of church construction in Muslim majority neighbourhoods; influencing anti-pornography legislation; and forcing the government to ban a number of musical and cultural events such as a concert by U.S. pop star Lady Gaga. They have also proven adept at strategically positioning themselves as key brokers for political parties and elites seeking to capture the perceived "Muslim vote", particularly as found in the broader conservative shift within mainstream Indonesian Islam over the past decade. As such, they have been able to punch far above their weight in terms of the ability to influence local government policies. The organization is relatively small in size, with an active national membership of at most 100,000 to 200,000.

The "anti-democracy" stance has become in effect a valuable and increasingly popular form of political capital. It is also not limited to Islamists, with a number of groups and individuals advocating various types of "democratic downgrading", from the ending of regional direct elections advocated by the Democrat Party, to the increasing expressions of sentimentality for the Suharto era. As Jacqui Baker has noted, the failure of President Yudhoyono to implement key reforms during his two terms, such as overhauls of the endemically corrupt judicial system, police force and military will leave in place a "framework for authoritarianism".[2] Considering the authoritarian credentials of a number of frontrunner presidential candidates for 2014, Indonesia's democratic future is by no means secure.

MUSYAWARAH, NOT DEMOCRACY

What is it about Indonesia's post-1998 democracy that apparently so reviles Islamists such as the FPI? And what do they see as their preferred alternative? In his book-length treatise, *Wawasan Kebangsaan: Menuju NKRI Bersyariah* (National Concept: Achieving a Unitary State of the Republic of Indonesia Ruled by Syariah Law), Habib Rizieq identifies the so-called "problem of democracy" in Indonesia as a problem of history requiring a return to what he argues are the Islamic foundations of the Indonesian republic and constitution. According to Rizieq, there was never any constitutional declaration that Indonesia was a "democratic state"; rather the fourth principle of the state ideology of Pancasila establishes the republic as a nation based upon *musyawarah* and *mufakat*, or consensus decision-making through deliberation, which he claims is an authentic Islamic tradition and the mode of governance practised by the Prophet Muhammad, or the "government of Allah". Unlike Islamist groups such as Hizbut Tahrir or the Majelis Mujahedin Indonesia, the FPI does not reject the Pancasila as a national ideology, but instead argues that its inherently Islamic foundations have been misinterpreted and subverted by the infiltration of Western notions of majority-rule democracy and values of liberalism and secularism which are all flawed human-created value systems.

The FPI insists that *musyawarah-mufakat* is a form of decision-making process fundamentally different from the "majority rules" logic of secular democracy which can be easily manipulated and guided by human weakness; and which results in the creation of rules and laws in direct conflict with Islam. Embracing *musyawarah* as both an Islamic principle of government and as a foundation of the Indonesian constitution would require an end to electoral democracy in its current form. The concept of *NKRI Bersyariah* articulated by Rizieq and the FPI occupies in this respect a middle-ground between Islamists who reject the constitution and the republic entirely, and that of secular and authoritarian nationalists who reject liberal forms of democracy but see no exclusivist place for Islam.

The second key point for the FPI is the need to re-include the Jakarta Charter in the Indonesian Constitution. The core of the charter was the addition of six words to the first principle of the Pancasila, where "Belief in Almighty God" is qualified with "the obligation to follow Islamic Syariah for all Muslims". In what the FPI considers to be a historical betrayal, the amendment was eventually dropped by nationalists including Sukarno and Hatta in the final drafting.

The FPI's stance then is nationalist rather than pan-Islamic, in so far as it reiterates the importance of the territorial integrity of the republic, and the centrality of the Constitution and the Pancasila. In recent times, it has engaged in overtly nationalistic demonstrations, for example, outside the Australian Embassy after revelations of spying on Indonesian government ministers, in what some suspect was a campaign to highlight its pro-nationalist credentials prior to the national legislative and presidential elections to be held in 2014.

In order to achieve its goal of *NKRI Bersyariah*, the FPI and its allies such as the Forum Umat Islam or FUI, have engaged in street protests and mobilizations, regular acts of vigilante violence, and aggressive advocacy around select issues strategically chosen to generate maximum publicity. They have also flirted with the possibility of directly contesting via the democratic system they reject. For example, in 2008, the FPI briefly debated forming its own political party. They argued that existing Islamic parties, such as the PKS, PKB and PAN, had already lost their way, compromising their values by forming alliances with secularists, or embracing non-Muslims as candidates. The spirit of a "revolutionary Islam", which concerned itself "only with the politics of Syariah, and not the politics of vested interests" was, in their view, no longer represented in the party system.[3] Eventually, the idea was dropped, as it was considered to involve too many compromises.

Rizieq has also been championed by the organization as a potential presidential candidate, together with a number of high-profile figures such as Cholil Ridwan, chairman of the Majelis Ulama Indonesia. The FPI's position that the nation should be led by Islamic religious scholars rather than politicians is one with obvious appeal to the MUI, with whom the organization has developed a mutually beneficial relationship as the "enforcer" of its often controversial fatwa. Perhaps the most significant of these was the 2005 fatwa declaring liberalism, secularism and pluralism as *haram* (sinful or forbidden in Islam). In many respects, the fatwa was a conservative reaction to the growing popularity of liberal streams of thought within mainstream Islamic organizations such as Nahdlatul Ulama and Muhammadiyah, exemplified in the minds of conservatives by the *Jaringan Islam Liberal*, or Liberal Islam Network. The FPI however took the anti-liberalism directive further, not just as a rejection of the spread of liberal ideas, but as a wholesale critique of the existing democratic system. If liberalism was *haram*, then liberal democracy must also be *haram*. The anti-liberal movement has subsequently grown to encompass a broad coalition of Islamist groups together with conservatives from mainstream Islamic organizations.

Earlier in March 2011, al-Jazeera revealed the existence of a document outlining the structure of a so-called Revolutionary Islamic Council. Compiled by former Hizbut Tahrir leader, head of the Forum Umat Islam and close confidant of the FPI, Muhammad Al Khathath, it was formulated as an Islamist "dream team". Al Khathath explained that in the wake of the Bank Century corruption scandal there was a sense that the government could collapse at any time; hence it was necessary to formulate an alternative government to fill any resulting power vacuum.

FPI figures feature prominently in the shadow cabinet, with Habib Rizieq as head of state, FPI spokesman and lawyer Munarman as Minister of Defence, and jailed radical cleric Abu Bakar Bashyir as part of a council of religious elders. Aside from Islamists, former New Order generals such as Tyasno Sudarto also featured in the shadow cabinet. While denying any knowledge of the document, Sudarto admitted to holding discussions with Islamist groups on the "future of the nation", as they both shared a desire for a return to the Pancasila as they understood it, and a rejection of moves towards liberal democracy. The document created a brief furore, and was considered by some in Yudhoyono's camp as evidence of a military-Islamist plot to topple the government. It may have been little more than wishful thinking on the part of Al Khathath. However, this episode indicated that there was a point of ideological connection between New Order apologists seeking to roll back democratic reforms and Islamists. Rizieq has at times publicly praised former dictator Suharto as "decisive" and "charismatic".

DEMOCRATIC MEANS TO AN UN-DEMOCRATIC END?

How then is the FPI situating itself in relation to the 2014 elections? In an official position statement released in August 2013, the FPI stated that the elections constituted a "period of dire emergency" for Indonesian Muslims, as it holds the danger that those who will gain control of the political reins could further the spread of apostasy (*kemurtadan*).[4] To this end, the FPI implores Muslims to choose candidates and support political parties that display a commitment to enforcing Syariah Law and reflecting the concerns of the *ummah*. Despite its rejection of democracy, the FPI encourages Muslims to participate in it as a means of ending it. As with most of its public pronouncements, the statement was also to advertise that the FPI was open to offering support to those willing to pay lip service to its pet issues.

The FPI has already indicated some of those whom it considers unacceptable candidates. An example is former general Wiranto and his political party Hanura, an initial sponsor of the FPI during his period as armed forces chief. This is ostensibly due to his objectionable public support for the hosting of the Miss World pageant in Indonesia. The FPI had strongly opposed the pageant with rowdy street demonstrations and threats of disruptions, resulting in the event being moved from Bogor in West Java to Bali. The pageant was also sponsored by Wiranto's vice-presidential candidate, the ethnic Chinese billionaire media mogul Harry Tanoesoedibjo, whom Rizieq has publicly referred to as an infidel and "pig", who needed to be "slaughtered and burnt".

The governor of West Java, Ahmad Heryawan, currently short-listed by the Islamist PKS as one of its five potential presidential candidates, is an FPI favourite. During his campaign for re-election in 2012, he had shown his amenability to making deals with the FPI, signing a political pledge that if returned to office he would outlaw Ahmadiyah and its activities in West Java. The strongest party support for the FPI has come from the Islamic PPP. The party's chairman and current Minister of Religion, Suryadharma Ali, has been a regular public advocate of the FPI, even extending an offer to its fiery public spokesman Munarman to run as a legislative assembly candidate. Questioned over the appropriateness of collaborating with a group infamous for its use of vigilante violence, Suryadharma argued that it was better than not to embrace radical organizations into the system where they could, in his words, "make a positive contribution". The PPP's reaching out to the FPI, as well as a number of other well-known Islamists, is part of an attempt to establish itself as a purely Islamic party, differentiating it from others such as the PKS who have supported non-Muslim candidates.

On the back of the FPI's announcement regarding the 2014 elections, Home Minister Gamawan Fauzi, who less than ten months earlier had threatened to forcibly disband the FPI via recently revised laws governing non-government organizations, followed Suryadharma's lead in stating in October 2013 that the FPI was now a "national asset" and that regional and national leaders should work in partnership with them. Prabowo Subianto, considered a potential presidential frontrunner, responded positively to Gamawan's call by suggesting that the FPI could and should be "embraced". In short, there has been a considerable degree of renewed interest in "engaging" with the FPI by political elites in the period leading up to the 2014 elections, which raises uncomfortable questions about their own commitment to democracy. It seems likely that part of the logic behind moves to form alliances with the FPI and other Islamist groups is a strategic calculation to secure votes from particular constituencies with minimal substantive concessions.

This needs to be situated in the context of predictions of increasing levels of nonparticipation and informal voting, or *Golput*.[5] Only 7.7 per cent in the first post-New Order multi-party elections in 1999, non-participation had risen to close to 30 per cent by the national elections of 2009. Some have estimated that rates of *Golput* in 2014 could reach 40 per cent or even as high as 60 per cent. The reasons behind the increase in *Golput* are strongly debated. After all, it is difficult to attribute agency to acts of non-participation. However, the general consensus is that it reflects a growing disillusionment with the substance of institutional democracy. The almost daily revelations of governmental corruption at every level have seen the initial post-authoritarian euphoria slowly transform into a cynical disinterest, even disdain, towards the electoral process. Appealing to conservative Islamists and their sympathizers entails fairly minimal political concessions, such as adopting a hard-line stance against soft political targets like religious minorities, with the potential to electorally mobilize groups ideologically disinclined to vote. This arguably appears as a potentially easier electoral path for some parties and candidates than, for example negotiating demands for increases to the minimum wage with the growing trade union movement; or developing coherent policies for reducing Indonesia's growing poverty levels. Groups such as the FPI also have potential use, in the words of former police chief Sutanto, as "attack dogs" that can be deployed against progressive or liberal social forces.

The main potential spoiler, from the FPI's perspective, is the immense popularity of Joko Widodo or Jokowi, the former mayor of Surakarta and current governor of Jakarta. Many expect that he will run as either a presidential or vice-presidential candidate, with most polls putting him far ahead of other candidates, aside from *Golput*. His party, the PDI-P, has remained one of the most openly hostile to the FPI and the least amenable to granting concessions or cutting deals with Islamist groups. The FPI has already butted heads with Jokowi's Jakarta administration, in particular the deputy governor Basuki Tjahaja Purnama, also known as Ahok, who publicly ridiculed Gamawan's suggestion of government-FPI collaboration. A similar rebuttal came from Ganjar Pranowo, the PDI-P governor of Central Java.

Some in Jokowi's inner circle have claimed that his popularity is undermining support for local Islamist groups such as the FPI in Jakarta, particularly amongst the urban poor who make up the bulk of the FPI's membership. The so-called Jokowi-effect, however, may also be overstated. Jokowi-endorsed candidates, for example, failed to win elections for governor in West Java and North Sumatra in 2013, losing in both cases to PKS-endorsed candidates.

Ultimately any failure to significantly shape the outcome or the policy orientation of the winners of the 2014 elections will be attributed to the nature of democracy itself and its system of "one person, one vote" where, in the words of Rizieq "the voice of a prostitute or an alcoholic is considered of equal value to that of an esteemed Ulama or Habib".

Notes

1. Arrahmah.com, "Habib Rizieq: Demokrasi lebih bahaya dari babi", 2 April 2013 <http://www.arrahmah.com/news/2013/04/02/habib-rizieq-demokrasi-lebih-bahaya-dari-babi.html>.
2. Jacqui Baker (2012), "Indonesia and Australia: what makes neighbours good friends?", East Asia Forum, 17 August 2012 <http://www.eastasiaforum.org/2012/08/17/indonesia-and-australia-what-makes-neighbours-good-friends/>.
3. Interview with Habib Rizieq, Jakarta, December 2012.
4. Arrahmah.com, "Sikap FPI Pemilu 2014: Darurat bagi umat Islam", 31 August 2013 <http://www.arrahmah.com/news/2013/08/31/sikap-fpi-pemilu-2014-darurat-umat-islam.html>.
5. Golput, or *Golongan Putih*, literally meaning "White group", refers to an election boycott movement started by intellectuals in the early 1970s to reject the rigged pseudo-elections of the New Order. It has since become shorthand for active or passive non-participation in elections, or the intentional casting of invalid votes, as a political statement.

6

GETTING TO KNOW THE CONTESTANTS OF THE 2014 INDONESIAN PARLIAMENTARY ELECTIONS

Ulla Fionna and Alexander R. Arifianto

INTRODUCTION

The upcoming 2014 parliamentary and presidential elections will be the most important yet for Indonesia. Voters will go to the polls to pick their parliamentarians on 9 April, and parties will be vying for support from an increasingly sceptical electorate.

Three elections after major political reforms were carried out, there are strong demands that the democratic transition should continue. The process seems to have stalled with corruption remaining rampant, the legal system still weak and corrupt, and the parliament approving bills that

Ulla Fionna is Fellow at ISEAS and Alexander R. Arifianto is Visiting Fellow at ISEAS. This article was first published on 10 March 2014 as *ISEAS Perspective* 2014/14.

compromise reform objectives. These, along with overall dissatisfaction towards President Susilo Bambang Yudhoyono's (SBY) performance, have fuelled the demand and even urgency, for change in the political leadership.

The parties still remain the gateway to political office at the central and local levels,[1] and party politicians elected into public office are often responsible for managing state or local budgets. Many of these officials are now either jailed, facing trials, or under investigation for corruption allegations.[2] Meanwhile, they are broadly criticized for being inefficient and unproductive.[3] Aside from all these, parties are generally poorly institutionalized — as clearly evidenced by the lack of clear platforms, and by the heavy reliance on particular figures and leaders for support and popularity.

As a result, the upcoming elections will be about which party has the most popular candidates. Parties have therefore been scrambling to identify those who can attract voters. This is made all the more necessary by the fact that specific platforms and party programmes are largely missing. The 2014 election is shaping up to be a race based on image and popularity. Increasingly, it is about those picked by parties to represent them.

THE PARTIES

Partai Nasional Demokrat
(Partai Nasdem, National Democratic Party)

Born as a mass organization, it declared itself a party on 26 July 2011. It lists Pancasila as its ideology, and it is the newest party that will be competing. This election is also its first. It was founded and chaired by Surya Paloh, an ambitious former Golkar official who owns Metro TV, the number one Indonesian television news network. While his wealth may boost Partai Nasdem's campaign efforts, its electoral chances are realistically small, as opinion polls predict that the party will only receive between 1 and 7 per cent of electoral votes in the legislative election[4] and his popularity as presidential candidate have been lingering around 1 and 2 per cent.[5] Serious problems emerged when Hary Tanoesoedibjo, another party pioneer and financier, left the party abruptly in January 2013; a move that was soon followed by party cadres at the national and local levels. Tanoesoedibjo's departure created a serious dent in the party's unity and thus its chances in the elections, particularly as he subsequently chose to join Partai Hanura (Partai Hati Nurani Rakyat, People's Conscience Party) and is now its vice-presidential candidate.

Partai Kebangkitan Bangsa (PKB, National Awakening Party)

The PKB is the official party affiliated with the Nahdlatul Ulama (NU), Indonesia's largest Islamic organization which has an approximate membership of 50 million Indonesians.[6] It was founded in 1998 by Abdurrahman Wahid, former NU chairman who went on to become Indonesia's first democratically elected President. After leading PKB for a decade, Wahid was ousted from his PKB chairmanship in 2008 by his own nephew, Muhaimin Iskandar, who took over as party chairman and has remained in that position till today. PKB's vote share has declined since the 1999 parliamentary election. While it won 12.6 per cent of the total votes that year, it only won 4.9 per cent of the votes in the 2009 election. Party leaders have nominated Rhoma Irama, a former Indonesian traditional pop (*dangdut*) singer and movie actor, to be its 2014 presidential candidate. However, two veteran politicians, Jusuf Kalla, former Indonesian Vice President and Mahfud, MD, former Chief Justice of the Constitutional Court, have also declared themselves presidential candidates for the party.[7]

Partai Keadilan Sejahtera (PKS, Prosperous Justice Party)

Coming out from the 2009 election as one of the surprise "winners", PKS' star quickly fizzled out after its former chairman, Luthfi Hasan Ishaaq was named as a suspect (and subsequently tried and jailed) in a corruption case. Arguably one of the few parties with a clear platform in Indonesia, PKS was known as a young Islamic party that demonstrated how Islam and democracy could be integrated. It offered a viable alternative to Muslim voters, and grew quickly from a small to medium-sized party. From

1.4 per cent in 1999, it gathered 7.3 (6th place) and 7.8 per cent (4th) in 2004 and 2009, respectively. However, the party's ambition to be one of the top three parties in 2014 seems rather unattainable after Luthfi was indicted and jailed. The corruption case dealt a severe blow to the party as it raises grave concerns about its standard of morality as a self-proclaimed religious party with a "clean" image. PKS has declared its decision to back current chairman Anis Matta as presidential candidate, but Anis' polygamous lifestyle may have worsened the party's image further. In any case, the possibility of PKS shifting its support to either former People's Consultative Assembly chairman Hidayat Nurwahid or West Java governor Ahmad Heryawan should not be completely ruled out.[8] Polls suggest that PKS will remain the strongest Islamist party. Anis is currently not a presidential contender, and the party will most likely gain around 3 per cent of votes, if not less.

Partai Demokrasi Indonesia–Perjuangan (PDI-P, Indonesian Democratic Party Struggle)

The PDI-P has been led since 1993 by its current chairman, former president Sukarno's daughter Megawati Sukarnoputri. PDI-P became Indonesia's ruling party in 2001 when Megawati succeeded the impeached President Wahid. However, she lost her re-election bid in 2004 and the party has been in opposition ever since. PDI-P's vote share declined significantly from a high of 33.7 per cent in 1999 (1st place), 18.5 in 2004 (2nd), to just 14 per cent (3rd) of the total votes in 2004.[9] Given the dissatisfaction towards the current government and the coalition of parties in power, some argue that the party may increase its vote share up to around 22 per cent in the upcoming elections.[10] However, there is deep disagreement within the party as to whom it should nominate as its presidential candidate. While stalwart Megawati supporters want her to be re-nominated, many PDI-P cadres want the honour to be given to the party's rising star, Jakarta Governor Joko Widodo (popularly known as Jokowi). While opinion polls suggest that Jokowi will win the presidential race in a landslide if he were the party's candidate,[11] Megawati is still reluctant to step aside and make way for him, a position that may jeopardize PDI-P's electoral success this year.

Partai Golkar (Golkar Party)

Defying great odds against its relevance in post-Suharto Indonesian politics, Partai Golkar remains one of the best organized parties in Indonesia — largely thanks to its extensive network built under the New Order regime (1966–98). It came in at second place in the 1999 elections with 22.4 per cent, and 21.6 per cent (1st place) in 2004, then declined to 14.5 (2nd place) in the 2009 elections. Its current chairman Aburizal Bakrie is a prominent business tycoon and a long-time party loyalist who successfully manoeuvred his way into the leadership position, and is now campaigning for presidency through the media outlets he owns.[12] Polls generally place him as the third most popular among the possible candidates, while surveys suggest the party will be one of the big winners in the parliamentary election.[13] However, some of the major issues that may very well deter voters from voting for this party is the Lapindo mud volcano fiasco in 2006, which implicated an oil and gas company he owns, and the ongoing corruption investigation of its cadre and Banten governor, Ratu Atut Chosiyah. Rather than distancing itself from the investigation, the party has chosen to throw support behind Chosiyah, and this may cost it dearly in the polls.

Partai Gerakan Indonesia Raya
(Gerindra Party, Great Indonesia Movement Party)

The Gerindra Party was revived in 2008 by retired Lieutenant General Prabowo Subianto,[14] a former son-in-law of Suharto who was implicated in but never charged for a number of human rights violations in Indonesia and East Timor during the 1990s. The party has become a vehicle to fulfil his presidential ambition, both in 2009 and in 2014. While it was only able to gain 4.5 per cent of votes during the 2009 legislative election, the party is expected to double its vote share this year, due largely to the increasing popularity of Prabowo, whom many polls are now predicting to be the second most popular potential presidential candidate after PDI-P's Jokowi.[15] Gerindra seems to be the most aggressive in their campaign over social media networks such as Facebook and Twitter, as it hopes to tap into the support of Indonesia's 47 million strong first-time young voters who are active online.[16]

Partai Demokrat (PD, Democratic Party)

Built for and on the figure of Susilo Bambang Yudhoyono (SBY), Partai Demokrat shot up to success in the 2004 election with 7.5 per cent votes (in 4th), and rapidly became the biggest party in the 2009 election with almost 21 per cent of the votes. Heavy dependence on SBY, followed by intense intra-party rivalry alongside large-scale corruption cases involving numerous party politicians. This means that the party will struggle for votes in April. Furthermore, SBY's strong personal grip and leaning towards dynastic politics in an intense intra-party competition for leadership, have resulted in the absence of an obvious successor. The ongoing convention to gauge which of the current eleven figures[17] competing for candidacy is the most popular, is strong evidence of the party's struggle. With some polls suggesting that the party is perceived as the most corrupt,[18] it is no wonder that it is predicted to gain only 4.7–6.12 per cent of votes.[19]

Partai Amanat Nasional (PAN, National Mandate Party)

Although it lists Pancasila as its ideology, PAN is officially affiliated with the Muhammadiyah, Indonesia's second largest Islamic organization which claims approximately 30 million members.[20] It was founded in 1998 by Amien Rais, the former Muhammadiyah chairman who was a leading opposition figure under Suharto. Vote share for the party has slightly declined from 7.1 per cent (5th place) of vote share in the 1999 legislative election, to just 6 per cent (5th) in the 2009 legislative election. Rais stepped down as party chairman in 2005 and its current chairman is Hatta Rajasa, the Coordinating Minister for Economic Affairs. His daughter is married to President Yudhoyono's son Edhie ("Ibas") Baskoro and he is also one of the president's closest aides. The party has officially endorsed Rajasa as its 2014 presidential candidate and is currently the most popular candidate from Islamist parties.[21] However, it is unlikely that it will be able to officially nominate him on the presidential ticket, as recent surveys indicate that PAN will only receive between 3 to 5 per cent of the vote share in the upcoming legislative election.[22]

Partai Persatuan Pembangunan
(PPP, United Development Party)

As one of only two other parties allowed to compete in New Order elections, PPP suffered heavy interference from the Suharto government. As an Islamic party, it was once stripped of its Islamic symbols and forced to adopt Pancasila and a more neutral symbol instead.[23] Although it has re-adopted the Ka'bah shrine as symbol and Islam as ideology, as with most other Islamic parties, PPP suffers from poor organization, and the lack of a strong leadership figure. After the retirement as party chairman of former Indonesian Vice President Hamzah Haz, the party has not been able to produce leaders of comparable calibre. Its current chairman cum candidate who is also the state minister for religious affairs, Suryadharma Ali does not stand a chance in these elections. PPP's votes have continued to decline since 1999, when it won 10.7 per cent (4th place), to 8.2 (4th place) in 2004, and only 5.3 (6th) in 2009, and polls currently suggest that the party will continue to struggle in the 2014 polls.

Partai Hati Nurani Rakyat
(Hanura Party, People's Conscience Party)

The Hanura Party was established in 2006 by retired General Wiranto, the former chief of the Indonesian Armed Forces during the time Suharto was removed from power in 1998. Like Nasdem, Democratic Party, and Gerindra, Hanura was perceived as a vehicle for the political ambitions of its founder, Wiranto, who had run as a presidential candidate in 2004 and as a vice presidential candidate in 2009. The party only received modest success in the 2009 legislative election, winning 3.8 per cent of the vote share and eighteen parliamentary seats. It hopes to significantly increase its vote share in the 2014 election by recruiting Hary Tanoesoedibjo, an Indonesian Chinese businessman who owns Rajawali Citra Television Network (RCTI) and two other Indonesian television networks, as its vice presidential candidate and chairman of its election strategy committee. Wiranto's chances as a presidential candidate vary quite widely,[24] and despite Tanoesodibjo's financial support, the party is only predicted to win about 4 to 7 per cent of the vote share in the upcoming legislative election.[25]

Partai Bulan Bintang (PBB, Star Crescent Party)

Rather similar to Partai Demokrat's reliance on SBY, PBB's influence is predominantly based on the figure of its founder and chairman Yusril Ihza Mahendra, a former Suharto speechwriter who reinvented himself as a pro-democracy activist during the Reformasi period. The fact that it was only added to the list of parties eligible to compete in the election after lodging an appeal demonstrates the struggle of the party to meet eligibility requirements. PBB gained 1.9 per cent of votes in 1999, 2.6 per cent votes in 2004, but this declined to 1.8 per cent in 2009. Polls are suggesting that its 2014 result will also be very poor, at about one percent or less. Yusril himself is not considered a popular presidential candidate at the moment, and his chances are considered very small.

Partai Keadilan dan Persatuan Indonesia (PKPI, Indonesian Justice and Unity Party)

The PKPI is a minor party founded in 1999 by a group of retired senior Indonesian army officers from the Suharto period. The party has never won more than 1.3 per cent of the vote share in the three parliamentary elections held since 1999. In the 2009 legislative election, it only won 0.9 per cent of the vote share. In order to improve its fortunes, in 2010 the party recruited retired Lieutenant General Sutiyoso, former Governor of Jakarta (1997–2007) as its new chairman. It remains to be seen whether the party can significantly improve its popularity under Sutiyoso's leadership.

CONCLUSION

It is clear that parties are still dominated by prominent and politically (sometimes also economically) powerful individuals, who use parties as vehicles to gain higher political offices (usually the presidency). This can be seen for most secular and Islamist parties (perhaps with the sole exception of PKS). Even parties that have a longer history of existence and are relatively well organized in the past (such as PDI-P and Golkar) are still dependent on prominent politicians as party leaders, who are reluctant to let anyone else challenge their dominance. If this trend continues, Indonesian parties will continue to become even less institutionalized and more personality-based.

The tendency of most Indonesian parties to form coalitions in order to gain access to financially lucrative cabinet positions and state enterprise directorships has made some scholars argue that they act like an economic cartel that leaves no real opposition in the parliament.[26] This cartel-like behaviour provides no real choice for Indonesian voters at the ballot box and leads to the disenchantment of many voters with respect to the political parties. This is why some scholars are predicting that as many as 37 per cent of eligible voters may abstain from voting altogether in the 2014 election.[27] The lack of institutionalization of political parties, their cartel-like behaviour, and increased voter apathy towards all political parties and most presidential candidates, have the potential to impede Indonesia's democratic transition even further.

Notes

1. Independent candidates can only run in local elections or pilkada (*pemilihan kepala daerah*) and most of the time they have lost to candidates endorsed by parties. Only party-endorsed candidates are eligible to run in presidential elections.
2. For instance, approximately 309 out of 542 Indonesian local government heads are currently under investigation for "numerous legal troubles", presumably corruption (Tempo.co, "309 Kepala Daerah Terlibat Masalah Hukum" (309 local government heads have legal troubles), 7 November 2013 <http://www.tempo.co/read/news/2013/11/07/063527834/309-Kepala-Daerah-Terlibat-Masalah-Hukum> (accessed 6 March 2013).
3. One study noted that they only pass a minimal number of bills amidst high numbers of absentees and low productivity. See <http://www.cdi.anu.edu.au/.IND/2010_11/D/2011_02_RES-WSC_INDON_HM_Seminar_DPR_CBR/2011_02_10_PP_HM.pdf>.
4. *Indikator*'s October survey suggested that Nasdem would get around 1 per cent, while *Kompas*' December survey in the same month said the party may get about 7 per cent. See *Indikator*'s survey at <http://indikator.co.id/news/details/1/35/

Laporan-Konferensi-Pers-Indikator-Efek-Jokowi-terhadap-Elektabilitas-Partai-danSimulasi-Elektabilitas-Capres-Potensial-di-2014>; *Kompas'* result can be studied in Elvan Dany Sutrisno, "Survei Kompas: PDI P No. 1, Demokrat Kian Terpuruk", detiknews, 9 January 2014 <http://news.detik.com/read/2014/01/09/110744/2462542/10/survei-kompas-pdip-no-1-demokrat-kian-terpuruk>.

5. See, for example, Muhammad Chandrataruna and Nila Chrisna Yulik, "Survei Pol-Tracking: Jokowi Masih Capres Pilihan Publik", vivanews, 22 December 2013 <http://us.politik.news.viva.co.id/news/read/468189-survei-poltracking--jokowi-masih-capres-pilihan-publik>, and Anggi Kusumadewi and Syahrul Ansyari, "Soegeng Sarjadi: Masyarakat Suka Tokoh Berwajah Memelas", vivanews, 13 September 2013 <http://us.politik.news.viva.co.id/news/read/443580-soegeng-sarjadi--masyarakat-suka-tokoh-berwajah-memelas/>.

6. Sumanto al Qurtuby, "Nahdlatul Ulama: Good Governance and Religious Tolerance in Indonesia", 15 January 2013 <http://blogs.nd.edu/contending modernities/2013/01/15/nahdlatul-ulama-good-governance-and-religious-tolerance-in-indonesia/> (accessed 4 March 2014).

7. Polling results of the three candidates suggest Kalla has the best chance of winning, with some putting him at nine and even 14 per cent. See, for example, Edward Panggabean, "Survei PDB: Jokowi Capres Paling Potensial", *liputan 6 news*, 6 Februari 2013 <http://news.liputan6.com/read/505726/survei-pdb-jokowi-capres-palingpotensial>, and "Survei Capres 2014 Terbaru: Jokowi No. 1 Lagi", tempo.co, 2 September 2013 <http://www.tempo.co/read/news/2013/09/02/078509618/Survei-Capres-2014-Terbaru-Jokowi-No1-Lagi>.

8. Among the three candidates, Hidayat pulls the biggest poll numbers, but only around one to two per cent or less. See, for example, Anggi Kusumadewi and Syahrul Ansyari, "Soegeng Sarjadi: Masyarakat Suka Tokoh Berwajah Memelas", vivanews, 13 September 2013 <http://us.politik.news.viva.co.id/news/read/443580-soegeng-sarjadi-masyarakat-suka-tokoh-berwajah-memelas/>, and "IRC: Elektabilitas Wiranto Bayangi Jokowi", jpnn.com, 23 October 2013 <http://www.jpnn.com/read/2013/10/23/197104/IRC:-Elektabilitas-Wiranto-Bayangi-Jokowi->.

9. The decline is largely due to voters' disenchantment with the party as it was embroiled in a number of high profile corruption scandals during the 2000s. For instance, see Viva News, "Proyek Taufiq Kiemas yang Disebut Wikileaks" [Taufik Kiemas' (Megawati Sukarnoputri's late husband) Projects Revealed by Wikileaks], 11 March 2011 <http://us.politik.news.viva.co.id/news/read/208870-proyek-taufiq-kiemas-yang-disebut-wikileaks> (accessed 4 March 2014).

10. Two of the latest polls predict high percentage of votes for PDI-P. *Kompas'*

December survey predicted a share of 21.8 per cent <http://news.detik.com/read/2014/01/09/110744/2462542/10/survei-kompas-pdip-no-1-demokrat-kian-terpuruk>, while Lembaga Survei Jakarta's January polls predicted that 19.8 per cent voters would support PDI-P <http://lembagasurveijakarta.com/survei-lsj-pdip-teratas-demokrat-melorot-di-posisi-6>.

11. Some of his poll numbers went as high as 47 per cent, with the lowest at 18. See, for example, Margareth S. Aritonang, "Jokowi Leads the Pack: Polls", *Jakarta Post*, 2 December 2013 <http://www.thejakartapost. com/news/2013/12/02/jokowi-leads-pack-polls.html>.

12. Bakrie's numerous media outlets include TV One, Indonesia's second highest-rated television news network and Viva News, an Indonesian-language online news portal.

13. See, for example, Ahmad Toriq, "Survei Charta Politika: Jokowi Capres Idaman, Mega Terjun Bebas", detiknews, 23 December 2013 <http://news.detik.com/read/2013/12/23/154257/2449686/10/survei-charta-politika-jokowi-capres-idaman-mega-terjun-bebas>, and "Survei Kompas: 43,5 Persen Responden Pilih Jokowi", kompas.com, 8 January 2013 <http://nasional.kompas.com/read/2014/01/08/0801224/Survei.Kompas.43.5.Persen.Responden.Pilih. Jokowi>.

14. The party was founded by General A.H. Nasution to compete in the 1955 Indonesian parliamentary election. However, it went defunct after President Sukarno dissolved parliament in 1960.

15. *Jakarta Post*, "Jokowi Leads the Pack: Polls", 2 December 2013 <http://www. thejakartapost.com/news/2013/12/02/jokowi-leads-pack-polls.html>.

16. *The Asia Foundation*, "Will Indonesia's Online Youth Shape 2014 Elections?", 16 October 2013 <http://asiafoundation.org/in-asia/2013/10/16/will-indonesias-online-youth-shape-2014-elections/> (accessed 4 March 2014).

17. They are: former army general and SBY's brother-in-law Pramono Edhi Wibowo, Supreme Audit Agency (BPK) member Ali Masykur Musa; Paramadina University's President Anies Baswedan; State-Owned Enterprises Minister Dahlan Iskan; Indonesian Ambassador to the US Dino Patti Djalal; former Indonesian Military (TNI) commander Endriartono Sutarto; Trade Minister Gita Wirjawan; Regional Representatives Council (DPD) Speaker Irman Gusman; House Commission I member and former Suharto's Minister of Youth and Sport Hayono Isman; parliament speaker and PD official Marzuki Alie; and North Sulawesi Governor Sinyo Harry Sarundajang.

18. See, for example, Septiana Ledysia, "Survei LSN: PD Paling Korup, Disusul Golkar dan PKS", detiknews, 24 March 2013.

19. The highest predictions was given by *Kompas*, but even that only predicted

around seven per cent votes for PD. *Kompas'* result can be seen in Elvan Dany Sutrisno, "Survei Kompas: PDI-P No. 1, Demokrat Kian Terpuruk", detiknews, 9 January 2014 <http://news.detik.com/read/2014/01/09/110744/2462542/10/survei-kompaspdip-no-1-demokrat-kian-terpuruk>.

20. Saiful Mujani and R. William Liddle, "Muslim Indonesia's Secular Democracy", *Asian Survey* 49, no. 4 (July/August 2009): 580.

21. His poll numbers vary between less than one to more than 14 per cent. The Centre for Strategic and International Studies (CSIS) April 2013 survey gave him 2.2 per cent, and Indonesian Institute of Sciences in May gave him 1.2 per cent. However, Political Climatology Institute and Indonesia Network Election Survey (INES) did surveys that excluded Jokowi's name in March 2013, and Prabowo came out the biggest winner with almost 20 per cent <http://klimatologipolitik.com/survei-lkp-prabowo-pertama-jokowi-tak-dianggap/> and even 39 per cent respectively <http://nasional.kompas.com/read/2013/04/07/19571264/Elektabilitas.Prabowo.Sebagai.Capres. Naik.Tajam>.

22. For example, both *Kompas* (in December) and Lingkaran Survei Indonesia (in January) predicted that PAN will only get around 3 per cent of the votes. *Kompas'* result can be accessed in Elvan Dany Sutrisno, "Survei Kompas: PDI-P No. 1, Demokrat Kian Terpuruk", detiknews, 9 January 2014 <http://news.detik.com/read/2014/01/09/110744/2462542/10/survei-kompas-pdip-no-1-demokrat-kian-terpuruk>.

23. The New Order government forced the party to drop Islam as ideology and adopt Pancasila, while the Ka'bah shrine symbol was replaced by a star.

24. His highest rating was in August 2013 when Political Climatology Institute put him under Jokowi's 19.6 per cent, at 18.5 per cent. Generally however, most polls rate him rather poorly, with around 5 to 7 per cent. See for example, Margareth S. Aritonang, "Jokowi Leads the Pack: Polls", *Jakarta Post*, 2 December 2013 <http://www.thejakartapost.com/news/2013/12/02/jokowi-leads-pack-polls.html>.

25. *Kompas'* December survey predicted a share of 6.6 per cent <http://news.detik.com/read/2014/01/09/110744/2462542/10/survei-kompas-pdip-no-1-demokrat-kian-terpuruk>, while Lingkaran Survei Indonesia's January polls put Hanura's chances at four per cent only <http://lsi.co.id/lsi/wp-content/uploads/2014/02/Konpers-2014-Pemerintahan-Golkar-atau-Pemerintahan-PDIP-Jan-2014.pdf>.

26. See Dan Slater, "Indonesia's Accountability Trap: Party Cartels and Presidential Power after Democratic Transition", *Indonesia*, 78 (October 2004): 61–92 and Kuskridho Ambardi, "The Making of the Indonesian Multiparty System: A Cartelized Party System and Its Origin", PhD Dissertation, Department

of Political Science, Ohio State University, 2008 <https://etd.ohiolink.edu/ap/10?0::NO:10:P10_ACCESSION_NUM:osu1211901025> (accessed 6 March 2014).

27. Tribunnews.com, "Peneliti LIPI Perkirakan Angka Golput Pemilu 2014 Bakal di Atas 30 Persen" [LIPI Researcher Predicts More than 30 per cent Indonesian Voters Will Abstain in the 2014 Election], 5 February 2013 <http://www.tribunnews.com/pemilu-2014/2014/02/05/peneliti-lipi-perkirakan-angka-golput-pemilu-2014-bakal-diatas-30-persen> (accessed 6 March 2014).

7

A SNAPSHOT OF THE CAMPAIGNING IN INDONESIA'S 2014 LEGISLATIVE ELECTIONS

Alexander R. Arifianto, Ulla Fionna and
Gwenael Njoto-Feillard

INTRODUCTION

Since 16 March, Indonesia has been in full campaign mode for its 2014 elections. This year's are the fourth legislative and the third direct presidential elections conducted after the country underwent its transition to democracy in 1998. The official campaign period for the national, provincial, and district-level legislative elections will continue until 5 April. After a cooling off period lasting a few days (*minggu tenang*), polling will take place on 9 April.

Alexander R. Arifianto is Visiting Fellow at ISEAS, **Ulla Fionna** is Fellow at ISEAS and **Gwenael Njoto-Feillard** is Visiting Fellow at ISEAS. This article was first published on 3 April 2014 as *ISEAS Perspective* 2014/20.

New methods are shaping the 2014 campaigns, especially at the grassroots level. First, parties are showing preference for the use of *blusukan* conducted by candidates to meet with individual voters. Literally meaning going through places in which passage is difficult (crowds, scrubs, narrow alleys, etc.), *blusukan* is now seen as an essential mode of campaign. This method is supposed to help voters to get to know their candidate at a more personal level. Voters can look for particular personal attributes, while candidates can show that they genuinely care about individual voters' concerns. Second, although money politics remains an integral part of the campaign approach, the way parties rely on it has changed. The cost of mobilizing voters for mass rallies (*pawai*) have become more expensive, and parties are now more careful about spending the money on them. Consequently, there are now less rallies and they are only reserved for visits by high-profile leaders. Furthermore, as most parties would be doing the same thing, any advantage that any party may gain from luring supporters with money is cancelled out. As such, money no longer has the kind of power it used to have for buying votes. The role that money will play on the polling day remains unclear.

THE INCREASING POPULARITY OF *BLUSUKAN*

In past elections, parties preferred a mass mobilization of members and supporters. They typically held mass rallies to draw supporters, usually by staging live music and other kinds of entertainment. This year things have clearly changed. Although parties still conduct these rallies, they are fewer in numbers, and are smaller. Rather, the most interesting aspect in this year's campaign is how the methods generally adopted by most political parties and legislative candidates (*calon legislative* or *calegs*) to reach potential voters within their legislative districts (*daerah pemilihan* or *dapil*) have changed. With mass rallies, it was the voters who showed up to participate. But now it is the candidates who have to make the effort to visit voters. In this sense, voters now have to be wooed and candidates are expected to demonstrate their willingness to serve them. Candidates are increasingly adopting a direct approach that is reminiscent of the approach used by political parties in Western democracies, which requires candidates to go directly to their constituents to sell themselves and their policies. This is also known as "retail politics".[1] In the Indonesian case, these new means seem to have been heavily inspired by the *"blusukan"* approach that Joko Widodo popularized during his campaign for the governorship of Jakarta Metropolitan Special Province in 2012. The current Jakarta governor, who has just been designated by the Indonesian Democratic Party Struggle (PDI-P) as its presidential candidate, is presently leading most poll surveys.[2] He has almost single-handedly developed the new ways of reaching out to voters which have become popular.

Indeed, parties are increasingly adopting *blusukan*-style events such as small-scale village town meetings and door-to-door visits by candidates to individual homes as their primary means to meet voters and seek their support. For instance, a candidate from the National Awakening Party (*Partai Kebangkitan Bangsa*, PKB) who is running for a regional legislative (DPRD) seat in the Sleman district (Central Java) states that he interacts with potential voters by attending events such as Islamic community prayers (*pengajian*), attending small group discussions with certain constituencies (e.g., farmers, factory workers, university students, etc.), carrying out door-to-door visits to people's homes, and posting advertisements/flyers in street corners and other strategic places.[3]

Many candidates believe their *blusukan*-style methods are the most effective means to reach potential voters at the grassroots level since voters are more likely to support those they know the best. Even though the official campaign period only started on 16 March, most candidates began their campaigns more than a year ago and have continuously campaigned in their respective districts ever since. Thus, many have developed relationships with people from their *dapil*, which they hope will translate into votes in the 9 April election. Voters indicate in turn that the candidate's character and perceived closeness to the voters are their primary selection criteria for the election. Voters tend to consider a candidate to be close to them if he or she lives within the community, attends campaign events in person instead of being represented by members of his/her campaign staffs (*tim sukses*), and is seen to be responsive to the community's concerns and needs.[4]

Thus, personality and character are an important variable in the campaigns. How the candidates directly interact with their constituents is a much stronger determinant of votes — while advertisement on television and banners posted on streets matter less.[5] This is rather ironic as Indonesian streets have been littered with a myriad of posters and banners of all sizes. Voters get much less information about candidates from these printed materials, which typically only contain simple catchy taglines along with a picture of the candidate's face, the symbol of his or her party, and the number in the ballot.[6] It is evident that *blusukan* is emerging as a more promising and effective method for candidates.

MONEY POLITICS IN THE LEGISLATIVE ELECTION

Money politics will still play an important role in the legislative election, but its role is also changing. Vote-buying by presidential and legislative candidates have become a common feature of post-*Reformasi* Indonesian elections since 1999.[7] However, what makes vote-buying in this year's elections different from previous elections is the extent to which it has become widespread and accepted. In areas we observed in our field study in Central and East Java, vote-buying activities were common. The practice has become so common that party officials and candidates openly admitted during interviews that it is unavoidable if they are to attract support for campaigns, and hopefully win votes as well.

For instance, when parties organize mass rallies, large sums are used to persuade supporters to flock to these events. These payments are usually called "*uang bensin*" (lit. gas money/transport allowance).[8] Other costs come from the printing of T-shirts, banners, and various essentials. However, as evidenced in Malang (East Java), such techniques sometimes have not even succeeded in mobilizing enough supporters to fill up a small basketball stadium.[9] A PKB rally in Malang even offered door prizes, but this still failed to draw a bigger crowd.[10] Thus, the recent shift away from mass rallies (*pawai*) also comes from the fact that these are not only expensive, but also probably not very effective.[11] In contrast, the Jokowi-style *blusukan* is cheaper and gains more sympathy than at the usually crowded, loud, and traffic-stopping rallies. As such, although the General Elections Commission (*Komisi Pemilihan Umum*, or KPU) has allocated a set of campaign dates and spots for each party, these have rarely been used — except when high-profile party leaders visit.[12]

Elections in Indonesia have become an expensive undertaking for parties and candidates alike. Direct elections, the current election system that allows thousands of candidates to run,[13] and lack of organizational prowess among parties have forced candidates to organize and fund their own campaigns. Lax of campaign finance regulations in Indonesia also allows for millions of dollars in donations to be funnelled to all major political parties from anonymous individuals and corporations, with virtually no legal restrictions.[14] A closer look at the various donations and contributions to parties reveals that many of them have established massive war-chests. As of early March 2014, all political parties have reported a combined campaign budget of Rp1.9 trillion (US$171 million).[15] Much of these funds are invested by the parties in both legal campaign activities (e.g., media advertisements, banners, and billboards) as well as in illegal ones (e.g., vote-buying).

In Sleman and also in Malang, officials from various parties have indicated that all their parties are engaging in vote-buying activities. Money politics in the districts has become so rampant that even candidates with extensive personal appeal who regularly use *blusukan* activities still feel obliged to engage in vote-buying activities to ensure that their supporters are not swayed by the money received from other candidates.[16] On average, it is estimated that candidates spend between Rp50,000 to Rp60,000 (US$4.2 to US$5) per voter.[17] Within the Sleman district, the largest expenditures spent by a PKB *caleg* is Rp900 million (US$75,000), while on average, PKB *calegs* incur between Rp300 and Rp500 million (US$25,000 to US$41,670) in campaign expenditures.[18]

However, the desired effect of such money politics seems to be diluted by the fact that voters are receiving similar amount of bribes from different parties. Parties and candidates realize that only a handful of voters whom they have bribed will actually vote for them in the end. Thus, they try to make estimations of how many votes they can expect. For example, the PKB Party in Yogyakarta estimates that on average, only 40 per cent of the voters that have received money from PKB *calegs* will actually vote for them in the April legislative election. This number increases to 60 per cent in villages where support for the party is considered very strong, and decreases to less than 20 per cent in villages where support for the party is weak.[19]

CONCLUDING REMARKS

The increased utilization of new direct campaign methods such as *blusukan* is forcing parties and legislative candidates to make their case directly to grassroots voters. As a result, these voters are increasingly demanding that candidates have strong personal appeal and demonstrate genuine care for the constituents. The advent of "retail politics" in Indonesia is creating a new breed of candidates who need to create and maintain direct contact with the community — while old-style politicians are increasingly perceived to be out of touch, and as desk-bound officials.

Unfortunately, money politics remain a troubling feature in this year's legislative election, as most parties and candidates continue to give out money to entice voters to support them during the campaign and also at the voting booth. It is even more troubling to see that this practice is no longer a taboo subject and that many politicians are willing to talk about it openly. Parties continue to use this method, not least because they have failed in developing solid organizational structures with clear platforms and programmes.

However, since many parties are opting for money politics, and none of them are left with an edge over the others, the effect of bribing voters remains unclear. By sticking to their own choice, voters may eventually force parties to abandon money politics or, at least, diminish its prominence in the Indonesian electoral process. It will thus be important to evaluate, after the legislative elections, whether parties and candidates still consider such investments to be really worthwhile.

Notes

1. For principles of the concept, see Judith S. Trent and Robert V. Friedenberg, *Political Campaign Communication: Principles and Practices* (New York: Praeger, 1991).
2. For instance, see Dave McRae, "Indonesian Politics in 2013: The Emergence of New Leadership?" *Bulletin of Indonesian Economic Studies* 49, no. 3 (2013): 292. For Jokowi's winning chances, see, for example, Margareth S. Aritonang, "Jokowi Leads the Pack: Polls", *Jakarta Post*, 2 December 2013 <http://www.thejakarta-post.com/news/2013/12/02/jokowi-leads-pack-polls.html> (accessed 31 March 2014).

3. Interview with Mohammad Alfuniam, *caleg* for the Sleman regional legislature (DPRD II) from the National Awakening Party (PKB), 19 March 2014.

4. Ibid. Each candidate usually has a team that supports his/her campaign — these are called *tim sukses*. Usually the bigger the constituents the bigger the *tim sukses* is.

5. For instance, see the Charta Politica Survey conducted on 1–8 March 2014, summarized in Bagus BT. Saragih, "TV ads 'not effective' in influencing voters", *Jakarta Post*, 26 March 2014 <http://www.thejakartapost.com/news/2014/03/26/tv-ads-not-effective-influencing-voters.html> (accessed 27 March 2014).

6. For instance, some of these banners and posters in Malang have taglines such as *"peduli wong cilik"* (care for the little people), *"berjuang untuk kesejahteraan rakyat"* (will fight for people's prosperity), and *"hidup mati bersama rakyat"* (life and death with the people).

7. See, for example, Vedi R. Hadiz, "Decentralization and Democracy in Indonesia: A Critique of Neo-Institutionalist Perspectives", *Development and Change* 35, no. 4 (September 2004): 697–718; Nankyung Choi, "Local Elections and Party Politics in Post-Reformasi Indonesia: A View from Yogyakarta", *Contemporary Southeast Asia* 26, no. 2 (2004): 280–301.

8. Some candidates in Malang (East Java) complained that even this has become more expensive. It costs them Rp25,000–30,000 (SG$3–4) for only one supporter, while in the previous campaign Rp10,000–15,000 (SG$2–3) was enough.

9. The Partai Amanat Nasional (PAN, or National Mandate Party) in Malang organized such a rally on 22 March 2014 and chairman Hatta Rajasa attended as the main attraction. However, only about 500 people showed up.

10. The prizes offered were a fridge and a gas stove. The rally was held on 21 March, and only around 500 people attended it.

11. Political parties often hire traditional Indonesian pop (*dangdut*) singers, TV actors and actresses, and attractive female dancers as free entertainment to the scores of people who attend the *pawai* rallies. Many participants are actually there for this sole purpose and barely listen to the stump speeches given by politicians.

12. These campaign spots are usually public stadiums. A drive through these locations in Surabaya, Malang, and Yogyakarta during our field trip reveals that they were not used for campaign events despite the fact that the spots had already been allocated to parties.

13. Voters typically have to cast their votes for the municipal, provincial, and national candidates. Each party has multiple candidates for each of these levels.

14. Marcus Mietzner, "Party Financing in Post-Soeharto Indonesia: Between State Subsidies and Political Corruption", *Contemporary Southeast Asia* 29, no. 2 (2007): 238–63.
15. The party with the biggest campaign fund is Gerindra with more than Rp306 billion (US$27 million). See "Ini Daftar Laporan Awal Dana Kampanye Parpol", *Kompas*, 2 March 2014 <http://nasional.kompas.com/read/2014/03/02/2124214/Ini.Daftar.Laporan.Awal.Dana.Kampanye.Parpol>.
16. In the words of the party official, "In real life, money is king. We cannot hope to gain any votes if we do not use money [to bribe them]." ("Pada kenyataannya, duit itu rajanya. Kita nggak bisa dapat suara kalau nggak pakai duit") (Confidential interview with a PKB party official from Yogyakarta, March 2014).
17. Confidential interview with a PKB party official from Yogyakarta, March 2014.
18. Ibid.
19. Ibid.

8

UNPACKING THE RESULTS OF THE 2014 INDONESIAN LEGISLATIVE ELECTIONS

Alexander R. Arifianto

INTRODUCTION

The recently concluded legislative election in Indonesia produced several unexpected results. The first one was the underperforming results of the opposition party the Indonesian Democratic Party–Struggle (Partai Demokrasi Indonesia–Perjuangan, PDI-P), which failed to capitalize on the popularity of its presidential candidate Joko Widodo (popularly known as Jokowi).

The party is estimated to have won only 19 per cent of the popular vote, far below the expected 25 to 30 per cent that had been predicted by a number of Indonesian public opinion surveys. Another unexpected result of the legislative election was the strong showing of Islamic political

---

Alexander R. Arifianto is Visiting Fellow at ISEAS. This article was first published on 17 April 2014 as *ISEAS Perspective* 2014/24.

parties,[1] which seem to have obtained a combined vote share of nearly 32 per cent. This reverses their poor results in the 2009 legislative elections and defies predictions made by pollsters and journalists that these parties were going to achieve even worse results in this election.[2]

This article unpacks the results of the Indonesian legislative election (*pemilihan legislative/pileg*) by focusing on these two key findings. Based on a comparison of estimated results from the current election with the final results from previous post-*Reformasi* elections (1999, 2004, and 2009), it is argued that:

a. Although PDI-P managed to achieve a significant vote gain in this election, it failed to capitalize on the popularity of its presidential candidate, Jokowi, due to the lack of television advertising, local-level campaigning of candidates, possible vote-buying at the grassroots level,[3] and internal rivalries between Jokowi supporters and those of PDI-P chairwoman Megawati Soekarnoputri, and;

b. The stronger-than-expected results of the Islamic parties should not be interpreted as evidence of political Islam gaining ground in Indonesia. Instead, this result can be attributed mostly to the parties' strategy to re-focus their campaign within their own primary constituencies.

EVALUATING PDI-P'S PERFORMANCE

Twelve national political parties competed in the 2014 legislative election,[4] and PDI-P was favoured to win big, especially after it nominated the popular Jakarta Governor Joko Widodo as its presidential candidate on 14 March 2014.[5] Opinion polls had expected the party to ride the wave of the "Jokowi effect" and comfortably pass the 25 per cent popular vote threshold, which would have enabled it to nominate its own presidential candidate without seeking coalition partners.[6]

However, although PDI-P managed to come ahead of all other parties, it only received approximately 18.94 per cent of the vote, falling far short of the 25 per cent threshold. Table 1 shows that PDI-P only managed to gain around 5 per cent of additional votes from the last legislative election (2009), far short of its all-time high of 33.7 per cent obtained in 1999.

TABLE 1
Vote Shares of Indonesian Political Parties, 1999–2014

Parties	1999	2004	2009	2014 (provisional)ᵃ
PDI-P	33.70%	18.50%	14.00%	18.94%
Golkar	22.40%	21.60%	14.50%	14.32%
Gerindra	N/A	N/A	4.50%	11.82%
Demokrat	N/A	7.50%	20.90%	9.66%
PKB	12.60%	10.60%	4.90%	9.19%
PAN	7.10%	6.40%	6.00%	7.48%
PKS	1.40%	7.30%	7.90%	6.92%
Nasdem	N/A	N/A	N/A	6.89%
PPP	10.70%	8.20%	5.30%	6.66%
Hanura	N/A	N/A	3.80%	5.44%
PBB	1.90%	2.60%	1.80%	1.61%
PKPI	1.01%	1.30%	0.90%	1.06%

Notes: a. Provisional data based on *CSIS-Jakarta Post Quickcount* results. At the time of writing, there are recounts and revotes being scheduled to take place in a number of polling stations. Final results are scheduled to be announced by the KPU on 6–7 May 2014.

Source: The General Election Commission (KPU) data (1999–2009); *The Jakarta Post — CSIS Quickcount* data (2014) (updated 11 April 2014).

Table 1 also shows that with the exception of incumbent President Yudhoyono's Democratic Party (PD), which loses approximately 11 per cent of its vote share compared to 2009, many of the parties competing in this year's election increased their vote shares compared to their 2009 results.[7] While the PDI-P managed to gain approximately 5 per cent of vote shares, its main rival, the Gerindra Party, managed to gain about 7 per cent of vote shares compared to its 2009 results. Gerindra's success can be attributed to the popularity of its leader, retired General Prabowo Subianto, who frequently asserted himself as a tough and decisive leader with a can-do attitude (unlike the image of incumbent President Yudhoyono) and to its aggressive social media campaign over the internet to attract the estimated 21 million-strong first time voters between the age of 17 and 21. Gerindra is considered to have the most extensive social media presence compared to other political parties.[8] The third finisher in this legislative election is the Golkar Party, which obtained 14.32 per cent of vote share this year, a slight decrease from its 14.50 per cent vote share in the 2009 election.

PDI-P's lower-than-expected electoral performance in this year's legislative election may be attributed to its failure to capitalize on the popularity of its presidential candidate, Jokowi, during the campaign season from 16 March to 5 April. The majority of PDI-P's television ads featured its chairman Megawati Sukarnoputri and her daughter, Puan Maharani, and not Jokowi.[9] The party only released advertisements featuring Jokowi during the final two days of the campaign. Even though this advertisement was also posted on social media sites such as Youtube, it only managed to attract a small number of online viewers.[10] As Jokowi himself indicates in his first post-election interview, the lack of television advertisements featuring him, and the barrage of negative advertisements by his political opponents (especially from the Gerindra Party) in social media may have prevented more voters from casting their ballots for PDI-P during the election.[11] Consequently, many voters did not see the connection between voting for PDI-P and Jokowi's presidential candidacy. Thus, these voters may have failed to support PDI-P during the legislative election.[12]

Another reason why PDI-P may have failed to win more votes in the legislative election is the fact that in this election, campaign messages were delivered through the efforts of individual legislative candidates (*calegs*) rather than through an organized strategy planned by the national party headquarters in Jakarta. Many *calegs* did not make use of the party structures during their campaign and often failed to mention which parties they came from when campaigning in their constituencies.[13] Vote-buying was also heavily used by all political parties in their grassroots-level (*blusukan*) campaigns and while its actual effects are very difficult to measure, it may have taken away some potential votes from PDI-P as well.[14]

Lastly, PDI-P seems to have been caught in an internal rivalry between Jokowi and Megawati Sukarnoputri's daughter, Puan Maharani, the chairwoman of the party's legislative election campaign committee. While the two have publicly denied it,[15] this may have contributed to the lack of enthusiastic support from Megawati towards Jokowi's presidential bid as well as the lack of campaign funds allocated by the party to support his campaign activities.[16] Although the two currently project a united front in their public appearances, any trace of internal rivalry needs to be resolved by the time the presidential campaign kicks into high gear in June. Otherwise, Jokowi may run into more difficulties in trying to beat whomever his opponents in the presidential elections may be.

ANALYSING THE RESURGENCE OF ISLAMIC PARTIES

Table 2 shows that the five Islamic parties[17] — the National Awakening Party (PKB), the National Mandate Party (PAN), the Prosperous Justice Party (PKS), the United Development Party (PPP), and the Crescent Star Party (PBB) — managed to win a 5.96 per cent compared to their combined results of 25.90 per cent in 2009. As most Indonesian analysts had predicted a further decrease in the Islamic parties' vote share following from their lacklustre results in 2009,[18] this year's results came as a surprise for many.

The National Awakening Party (Partai Kebangkitan Bangsa, PKB), which is affiliated with the Nahdlatul Ulama (NU), Indonesia's largest Islamic

TABLE 2
Vote Shares of Indonesian Islamic Parties, 1999–2014

Parties	1999	2004	2009	2014[a]
PKB	12.60%	10.60%	4.90%	9.19%
PAN	7.10%	6.40%	6.00%	7.48%
PKS	1.40%	7.30%	7.90%	6.92%
PPP	10.70%	8.20%	5.30%	6.66%
PBB	1.90%	2.60%	1.80%	1.61%
Total	33.70%	35.10%	25.90%	31.86%
Average Vote Share (1999–2014)				31.64%

Note: a. Provisional data based on CSIS-Jakarta Post Quickcount results. Final results will be announced by the KPU on 6–7 May 2014.
Source: The General Election Commission (KPU) data (1999-2009); *The Jakarta Post* — *CSIS Quickcount* data (2014) (updated 11 April 2014).

organization, managed to gain approximately 9.2 per cent of vote share this election, nearly doubling its performance of 4.9 per cent obtained in 2009. This makes it the biggest winner among the five Islamic parties.

However, concerns expressed in several news reports regarding the rise of influence among Islamic parties are overblown.[19] Table 2 shows that the average vote shares of the parties in legislative elections conducted between 1999 and 2014 is 31.64 per cent. This indicates that the parties' 2014 combined vote share of 31.86 per cent is only slightly above the average of the parties' electoral performances since 1999.

The strongest explanation for the success of these parties in this election lies in their campaign strategy to focus on their primary constituencies — most notably members of Islamic organizations that supported these parties when they were first founded (e.g., NU for PKB, Muhammadiyah for PAN, etc.). This is especially so in the case of PKB, which sought to recover from its record low vote share of 4.90 per cent in 2009 by actively remobilizing its voter base within its main constituency, e.g. the millions of NU members and sympathizers.

PKB's dismal result in the 2009 election was primarily attributed to the internal divisions within its leadership.[20] In May 2008, the late Abdurrahman Wahid, PKB's founder and first general chairman, was ousted from his position by his own nephew, Muhaimin Iskandar. As a result, the party split into two factions.[21] In addition to this split within PKB, a second NU-affiliated party, the National Ulama Awakening Party (Partai Kebangkitan Nasional Ulama, PKNU) was founded in November 2006 by a group of conservative NU clerics (kyai) led by KH Ma'aruf Amin.[22] While PKNU only won 1.5 per cent of vote share during the 2009 election, many PKB politicians have blamed the party for taking away a sizable number of votes from NU members in 2009, further contributing to PKB's poor results in that year's election.[23]

To strengthen PKB's voter base within NU, legislative candidates (caleg) visited villages where NU is known to have a strong representation. In their campaigns, these caleg reminded NU members and sympathizers that their organization shared historical roots with PKB and that both were defending traditionalist Islamic teachings. NU was founded in 1926 by KH Hasyim Ash'ari, while PKB was founded by his grandson, Abdurrahman Wahid in 1998 to represent the NU community in the realm of politics. Hence, according to this argument, the only option for NU members is to vote for PKB, the only party that truly represents them.[24]

At the national level, Muhaimin Iskandar and his lieutenants have been working to mend ties between PKB and the NU leadership, which have not had harmonious relations with the party since around 2004.[25] In April 2011, Iskandar managed to win the endorsement of the current NU chairman, KH Said Aqil Siradj, to support PKB in its political campaigns, despite NU's official position that it is a politically neutral civil society organization.[26] In addition to his endorsement, Said Aqil made numerous campaign appearances in PKB events, with a common tagline that PKB is "a fundamental part of NU and should be supported by all NU members".[27] Iskandar has also approached disgruntled PKB politicians such as the former Indonesian Constitutional Court Chief Justice, Mahfud MD,[28] and former Minister of Woman's Empowerment, Khofifah Indah Parawangsa, and succeeded in regaining they formal support for PKB.[29] PKB leadership's reconciliation with the NU leadership and formerly disgruntled PKB politicians has unified the two organizations for the first time since 2004, thereby potentially increasing the support of NU members for PKB in this year's legislative election.

NU's support for PKB's electoral endeavors has also been bolstered by Iskandar's ability to bring Rusdi Kirana, an Indonesian Chinese, and founder and chief executive officer of Lion Air, Indonesia's largest budget airline, to become the party's chief financial patron in January 2014.[30] A month later, Kirana established the "NU-Lion partnership," which is providing hundreds of thousands of US dollars as financial assistance to support the economic development of NU Islamic schools (*pesantren*) throughout East and Central Java, the primary stronghold of NU. In the process, he has been able to gain political support from NU clerics and their students (*santri*) who are running these schools.[31] He also provided donations to buy advertisements for PKB and support its local campaigns in NU strongholds in East and Central Java in March 2014.[32] Kirana's generous financial support to NU's *pesantren* coffers and to PKB's campaign efforts to win back NU members' votes at the grassroots level may have contributed to the increase in the party's vote share by 4.29 per cent this year.

There are indications that similar strategies were pursued by other Islamic parties in their campaigns as well. For instance, in light of the "cattle meat imports" corruption scandal which implicated a number of high ranking PKS leaders and politicians, the party has strengthen its support among its loyal and highly motivated cadres. PKS chairman Anis Matta has promoted a grand narrative in his public speeches that the corruption allegation against PKS politicians was part of a political conspiracy conducted by unnamed political opponents to undermine and destroy the party.[33] This narrative seems to have consolidated support among the party's cadres and sympathizers, giving them a common and elusive enemy that they should fight against by maintaining the party's unity.[34] Another strategy that seems to have worked is PKS's various charitable initiatives to help poor citizens and victims of natural disasters at the grassroots level.[35] This aimed to strengthen the bond between cadres and the party and negate the effects of the various scandals faced by party officials. These strategies seem to have worked, judging from the fact that PKS obtained a vote share of 6.92 per cent, approximately 1 percentage point below its all-time high vote share of 7.90 per cent obtained in 2009. However, this is still far higher than the predictions made by several polling organizations.[36]

CONCLUDING REMARKS

Two lessons can be drawn from the preliminary results of Indonesia's 2014 legislative election. First, the enormous popularity of a party's presidential candidate is not a guarantee for the party to win the legislative election. The PDI-P failed to effectively ride on Jokowi's popularity to gain more votes in the *pileg*. Lack of advertisements promoting Jokowi's candidacy during the campaign period, the barrage of negative campaigns from his political opponents, the effects of grassroots campaigning and vote-buying, and the internal rivalry between Jokowi's supporters and Megawati Sukarnoputri's supporters, seem to be the factors contributing to the party's lower-than-expected performance.

Second, the resurgence of Islamic parties' combined vote share should not be interpreted as a sign that political Islam is enjoying increased support from the Indonesian electorate — at least not just yet. Rather, indications suggest that this is the result of these parties' efforts at consolidating support among their primary constituencies.

It remains to be seen whether these parties will be able to gain additional votes outside their own primary constituencies in future elections and whether they will be able to collectively increase their influence within Indonesian politics.

Notes

1. "Islamism" considers Islam as not only a religion, but a political ideology, which is embodied in the ideal of the Islamic state and/or the application of Islamic law. Interpretations can vary: from "pluralist" and "adaptative" parties, such as the PKS, to more "conservative" ones, as in the case of the PBB.
2. For a poll that shows lower returns for Islamic parties, see Centre for Strategic and International Studies (CSIS, "Amidst the 'Jokowi Effect.' Vacillitating Voters and An Unfinished Contestation", 31 March 2014 <http://www.csis.or.id/post/press-release-csis-national-survey-march-2014>, pp. 5 and 13 (accessed 11 April 2014). For an example of media accounts, see Joe Cochrane, "Memo from Indonesia: In a Nation of Muslims, Political Islam is Struggling to Win Votes", *New York Times*, 7 April 2014 <http://www.nytimes.com/2014/04/08/world/asia/political-islam-indonesia.html?smid=fb-share&_r=0> (accessed 14 April 2014).
3. For a snapshot of grassroots (*blusukan*-style) campaigning and vote-buying, see Alexander R. Arifianto, Ulla Fionna, and Gwenael Njoto-Feillard, "A Snapshot of the Campaigning in Indonesia's 2014 Legislative Elections", *ISEAS Perspective* No. 20 (3 April 2014) <http://www.iseas.edu.sg/news_content.cfm?news_id=759A5157-0308-7E53-C4CAC0775536FBAA> (accessed 14 April 2014).
4. For a comprehensive profile of the 12 national political parties competing in this year's legislative election, see Ulla Fionna and Alexander R. Arifianto, "Getting to Know the Contestants of the 2014 Indonesian Elections", *ISEAS Perspective* No. 14 (10 March 2014) <http://www.iseas.edu.sg/research-output.cfm?category_id=63EF7BB0-1A64-6F37-E42E34D167B97E98&status=past> (accessed 11 April 2014).
5. Public opinion polls taken within the past year have indicated that Jokowi will beat any other presidential candidates (such as retired General Prabowo Subianto from the Gerindra Party) in a landslide. For instance, the latest survey conducted by the reputable Center for Strategic and International Studies (CSIS) predicts Jokowi will beat Prabowo 54.3 per cent to 28.3 per cent in a two-way electoral race. See CSIS, "Amidst the 'Jokowi Effect.' Vacillitating Voters and

An Unfinished Contestation", 31 March, 2014 <http://www.csis.or.id/post/press-release-csis-nation-al-survey-march-2014>, p. 25 (accessed 11 April 2014).

6. CSIS estimated that while without a clear presidential candidate, PDI-P would have only obtained 20 per cent of the vote share, it would have acquired 33 per cent if Jokowi was declared as its presidential candidate. See CSIS (2014), op. cit., pp. 5 and 13.

7. Parties that receive less vote shares this year compared to their 2009 election results are: Demokrat (11.24 per cent less), Golkar (0.18 per cent less), PKS (0.98 per cent less), and PBB (0.19 per cent less).

8. Alexandra Hearne, "I Tweet and I Vote: Indonesia's 2014 Elections and Social Media", *Radio Australia*, 3 April 2014 <http://www.radioaustralia.net.au/international/2014-04-02/i-tweet-and-i-vote-indonesia%E2%80%99s-2014-elections-and-social-media/1285632> (accessed 11 April 2014).

9. See <http://www.youtube.com/watch?v=0JS1lALc58E>, for an example of Megawati-Puan Maharani television ad (uploaded 10 March 2014). It is seen by 7,215 Youtube viewers as of 14 April 2014.

10. The PDI-P ad featuring Jokowi can be viewed at <http://www.youtube.com/watch?v=stKym4_7qtQ&feature=share> (uploaded 2 April 2014). It is only viewed by 550 Youtube viewers as of 14 April 2014.

11. Josua Gantan and Kennial Caroline Laia, "Joko: 'Attacks,' Poor Marketing, Have Hurt PDI-P", *Jakarta Globe*, 11 April 2014 <http://www.thejakartaglobe.com/news/joko-attacks-poor-marketing-hurt-pdi-p> (accessed 12 April 2014).

12. This is based from the observation of an ISEAS Indonesian Studies programme's staff on the election day at the Indonesian Embassy in Singapore, 6 April 2014. Many voters whom had intended to vote for Jokowi were disappointed that his picture was not featured on the ballot. Some of them went home afterwards without voting for any party (Conversations with Maxenius Tri Sambodo, 7 April 2014).

13. Edward Aspinall, "Why Was the Jokowi Effect Limited?", *New Mandala*, RSPAS, Australian National University, 10 April 2014 <http://asiapacific.anu.edu.au/newmandala/2014/04/10/why-was-the-jokowi-effect-limited/> (accessed 14 April 2014).

14. For an account on vote-buying at the grassroots level during the campaign season and its potential effects, see Alexander R. Arifianto, Ulla Fionna, and Gwenael Njoto-Feillard, "A Snapshot of the Campaigning in Indonesia's 2014 Legislative Elections", *ISEAS Perspective* No. 20 (3 April 2014) <http://www.iseas.edu.sg/news_content.cfm?news_id=759A5157-0308-7E53-C4CAC0775536FBAA> (accessed 14 April 2014).

15. *Jakarta Post*, "PDI-P Nixes Jokowi/Puan Rift Claims", 13 April 2014 <http://

www.thejakartapost.com/news/2014/04/13/pdi-p-nixes-jokowipuan-rift-claims.html> (accessed 14 April 2014).

16. Hans David Tampubolon, "Infighting Could Ruin Jokowi's Bid", *Jakarta Post*, 11 April 2014 <http://www.thejakartapost.com/news/2014/04/11/infighting-could-ruin-jokowi-s-bid.html> (accessed 14 April 2014).

17. In this article, Islamic parties are defined as any whose "platform and ideologies openly states Islam or draws their main support from Muslims or Muslim organizations" (Muhtadi 2012, p. 204; Baswedan 2004, p. 672). Muhtadi and Baswedan's definition is used in this article because conservative Muslim clerics and activists can be found in all Islamic parties, even in those with pluralist (Pancasila-based) platform such as PKB and PAN.

18. For instance, CSIS March 2014 survey was predicting a combined vote share between 12.30 per cent (with Jokowi as a declared PDI-P presidential candidate) and 19.70 per cent (without Jokowi as PDI-P candidate) for the five Islamic parties. See CSIS, "Amidst the 'Jokowi Effect.' Vacillitating Voters and An Unfinished Contestation", 31 March 2014 <http://www.csis.or.id/post/press-release-csis-national-survey-march-2014>, pp. 5 and 13 (accessed 11 April 2014).

19. For instance, see Otto and Schornhardt, op. cit. and Agence-France Presse, "Islamic Parties Bounce Back in Muslim-Majority Indonesia's Parliamentary Elections", *South China Morning Post*, 11 April 2014 <http://www. scmp.com/news/asia/article/1475955/islamic-parties-bounce-back-muslim-majority-indonesias-parliamentary> (accessed 14 April 2014).

20. Interviews with PKB *calegs* and politicians in Yogyakarta indicate they blame their party's 2009 losses on the internal split within PKB during this time. Interviews with Sukoyo, PKB *caleg* for the Yogyakarta Provincial Council (DPRD I), Yogyakarta, 19 March 2014, and with Muhammad Kholiq, PKB Party Chairman for the Sleman District, Sleman, 20 March 2014.

21. After a two-year legal fight, Iskandar's faction finally prevailed over Wahid's after the Indonesian Supreme Court ruled in July 2010 that the former was the legitimate leader of the party and not the latter. Wahid passed away on 30 December 2009 and most of his former supporters eventually went back to support Iskandar's faction.

22. Ma'aruf Amin is also a member of the Indonesian Ulama Council (*Majelis Ulama Indonesia, MUI*), Indonesia's semi-official *fatwa*-making Islamic council, and is now the organization's Vice-Chairman.

23. Interview with Muhammad Kholiq, PKB Party Chairman for the Sleman District, Sleman, 20 March 2014.

24. Interviews with Sukoyo, PKB *caleg* for the Yogyakarta Provincial Council

(DPRD I), Yogyakarta, 19 March 2014, and with Muhammad Kholiq, PKB Party Chairman for the Sleman District, Sleman, 20 March 2014. Also see the campaign speeches made by Mr Sukoyo and Mohammad Alfuniam, PKB *caleg* for the Sleman regional legislature (DPRD II), on their joint campaign appearances, 20 March 2014.

25. The split between PKB and NU can be traced back to the feud between PKB's founder Abdurrahman Wahid and then NU chairman Hasyim Muzadi in 2004. The latter refused to support the former's bid for the Indonesian presidency. Instead, Muzadi became Megawati Sukarnoputri's Vice-Presidential nominee. For further information, see Eunsook Jung, "Taking Care of the Faithful: Islamic Organizations and Partisan Engagement in Indonesia", PhD Dissertation, Department of Political Science, University of Wisconsin-Madison, August 2009.

26. Investor Daily Indonesia, "Said Aqil: PBNU Siap Dukung PKB" [Said Aqil: NU Leadership Board is Ready to Support PKB], 31 January 2011 <http://www.investor.co.id/home/said-aqil-pbnu-siap-dukung-pkb/4526> (accessed 12 April 2014).

27. An example of Said Aqil's campaign speeches can be found at <http://www.youtube.com/watch?v=Jdx7laV4flo> (uploaded 16 March 2014), (accessed 12 April 2014).

28. Mahfud, MD is one of PKB's presidential candidates in the 2014 presidential election, along with former Indonesian Vice-President Jusuf Kalla and traditional pop (*dangdut*) singer and movie actor Rhoma Irama.

29. A PKB advertisement featuring these two politicians can be found at <http://www.youtube.com/watch?v=cUsT7tlowb4> (uploaded 21 March 2014), (accessed 12 April 2014).

30. Kirana was immediately made PKB's Deputy Chairman, despite the fact that he is an Indonesian of Chinese descent and a non-Muslim. Greg Fealy, "The Lion of PKB, Rusdi Kirana", *New Mandala*, RSPAS, Australian National University, 31 March 2014 <http://asiapacific.anu.edu.au/newmandala/2014/03/31/the-lion-of-pkb-rusdi-kirana/> (accessed 12 April 2014).

31. Fealy (2014), op. cit.

32. Ibid.

33. Sabrina Acil, "Anis Matta Tuding Ada Konspirasi Besar untuk Serang PKS" [Anis Matta Alleges a 'Great Conspiracy' to Attack PKS], Kompas.com, 1 February 2013 <http://nasional.kompas.com/read/2013/02/01/16172470/Anis.Matta.Tuding.Ada.Konspirasi.Besar.untuk.Serang.PKS> (accessed 12 April 2014).

34. Masdarudin, "Konspirasi: Strategi PKS Menjadi Penguasa" [Conspiracy: PKS Strategy to Become a Ruler], Kompasiana, 2 April 2013 <http://politik.

kompasiana.com/2013/04/01/konspirasi-strategi-pks-menjadi-pengua-sa-547562.html> (accessed 12 April 2014).
35. During our fieldwork in March 2014, various PKS cadres in Jakarta and Malang have indicated the success of the party to continue holding various activities and charities. These cadres demonstrated strong commitment towards seeing the party through the various troubles.
36. For instance, the CSIS March 2014 survey predicted that PKS was only supposed to receive between 2.90 and 3.40 of vote shares in the April legislative election. See CSIS, "Amidst the 'Jokowi Effect.' Vacillitating Voters and An Unfinished Contestation", 31 March 2014 <http://www.csis.or.id/post/press-release-csis-national-survey-march-2014>, pp. 5 and 13 (accessed 11 April 2014).

9

INDONESIA'S 2014 LEGISLATIVE ELECTIONS
The Dilemmas of "Elektabilitas" Politics

Max Lane

INTRODUCTION

On 9 April 2014, around 200,000 people stood for election to 20,257 seats in the Regional and Provincial Legislative Councils (DPRD), the House of Representatives (DPR) and the Regional Representatives Council (DPD). Of these, 6,607 candidates from twelve parties competed for the 560 seats in the DPR, while the remainder ran for the 132 seats in the DPD, the 2,137 provincial seats and the 17,560 regional seats. There are 1,344 new seats, mostly in the regional parliaments and 123 in provincial parliaments.

Max Lane is Visiting Fellow at ISEAS, Lecturer in Southeast Asian politics and history at Victoria University, and Honorary Associate in Indonesian Studies at the University of Sydney. He has been in Indonesia watching the election process. This article was first published on 23 April 2014 as *ISEAS Perspective* 2014/25.

One week after the elections, more and more reports have surfaced of cheating during vote counting. Most of the reports are about switching counting of ballot papers for one candidate to another for money. This is possible with the bribery of election officials. Initially, complaints came from candidates who had been unable to mobilize enough supporters to be scrutinizers at the very large number of voting centres in each constituency. Their ballot papers were especially vulnerable. If those who lost votes due to cheating can document this, there may be a round of court cases disputing votes in different constituencies. It is difficult to know the extent of cheating at this time, but it is unlikely to change the overall picture presented by the election results.

WHAT HAVE THE ELECTIONS REVEALED?

Overall, the elections have confirmed the alienation between the mass of the population and the existing parties.

GOLPUT the Winner

Most election analysts are confirming a formal absentee voter rate (GOLPUT) at 34 per cent, up from 29 per cent in the 2009 elections.[1] This only includes the percentage of registered voters who did not vote. It does not include people who are eligible to register to vote but did not. Nor does it include spoilt votes.[2] It is probable that the real absentee vote is at least 40 per cent, i.e., at most only 60 per cent of the population voted.

There was a massive television advertising campaign, backed also by the party leaders, urging people not to "GOLPUT". On Election Day, television hosts as well as politicians were still confident that there would be a drop in GOLPUT. Moreover, there was the assumed impact of the presidential candidature of Joko Widodo, namely, that his popularity would *automatically* result in a higher voter turnout. This assessment failed to take into account the shallowness of Widodo's populism.[3]

Absentee voting either as a form of protest or a manifestation of lack of interest in the existing parties has a long history. The word GOLPUT, an acronym of Golongan Putih (White Group), goes back to 1971 and the first protests against electoral manipulation. The steady upward trend in

GOLPUT was what required an intense *Don't GOLPUT* campaign, but to no significant avail.

In fact, during 2013 there were elections for regional and provincial heads in nine different provinces, with all candidates being associated with the same parties standing in April. GOLPUT non-voting ranged from highs of 51 per cent in North Sumatra, 49 per cent in Central Java and 44 per cent in Bandung, to a best case scenario of 25 per cent in Bali. Others hovered around 35–37 per cent.[4] Most of the private polling was indicating 60 per cent distrust in all parties.[5]

The one apparent exception to the limited impact of the "Jokowi effect" is the GOLPUT and PDI-P vote in Solo city, where Widodo had been mayor between 2005 and 2012. PDI-P won 56 per cent of the votes. There, GOLPUT was down to 26 per cent. 56 per cent is a big increase on PDI-P's 2009 vote of 32 per cent, but considerably lower than Widodo's own remarkable 91 per cent vote share when he stood for a second term as mayor in 2010. It was winning that 91 per cent vote share that boosted his standing as a national figure and gave him the opportunity to make a bid for the governorship of Jakarta and eventually win it. The PDI-P also did better in Jakarta with 30 per cent of the vote, but there may be more factors at play than a simple "Jokowi effect".

Low Party Votes

No party received a vote share that allowed it to say that it was a nationally popular party. PDI-P is now often exaggeratingly called the "winner". The PDI-P "won" with just under 20 per cent of the vote, which — given that only 60 per cent of the eligible population voted — represented a mere 12 per cent of eligible voters.[6] This is hardly a win and actually gives the PDI-P no significant head-start over the "runners-up", Golkar at 15 per cent (i.e. 9 per cent of eligible voters) and GERINDRA at 11 per cent (i.e. 6.6 per cent of eligible voters). All of the other nine parties scored even less support.[7] The only thing which allows the PDI-P to behave as an actual winner is that its presidential candidate, Widodo, is scoring the highest in all the polls.

The PDI-P was clearly shocked by its low vote share.[8] Although it has increased from 14 per cent in 2009, throughout 2013 it was scoring at least 20 per cent and had climbed above that in opinion polls since the announcement of Widodo as its presidential candidate on 14 March.[9] On the afternoon of Election Day, appearing on Metro TV, Ganjar Pranowo, PDI-P figure and Governor of Central Java, was still insisting that the PDI-P would get 27 per cent of the vote share. The PDI-P was assuming that with at least 25 per cent of the vote share, it would not need to form a coalition with any other party to formally nominate Widodo in May. The failure to get anywhere near 25 per cent of the vote share has forced the PDI-P to rapidly seek a partner to nominate Widodo. PDI-P and Widodo quickly secured the support of tycoon and former GOLKAR heavyweight but now founder and chairperson of the Nasional Demokrat (NasDem), Surya Paloh. Nasdem received around 6.8 per cent of the votes, so a PDI-P-Nasdem coalition was just enough to meet the 25 per cent criterion and get Widodo nominated as a presidential candidate.

The low vote that the PDI-P received despite Widodo's popularity itself must be read as another manifestation of the alienation of the mass of the people from the parties. This picture is reinforced by the fact that all of the parties received such low votes. While the PDI-P found that its celebrity candidate could not stir voters into action, neither did any of those parties blessed with billionaire tycoons as backers and big budgets (GOLKAR, GERINDRA, NASDEM, HANURA) do any better. Islamic parties, with the benefit of access to the huge network of mosques, did not show impressive results either.

There was also little visible spontaneous participation in campaign activities. In the rallies and motorcades that I witnessed in Central Java and Jakarta, it was clear that only paid-up party supporters were involved. Television and social media photographs of campaign activities showed crowds that were inevitably all dressed in party colours.

ELECTABILITAS, EMPTINESS AND ITS IMPACT

The PDI-P nominated Widodo as their presidential candidate in March before the legislative elections in the hope that it would boost their vote share. This was their only strategy, although some advertising also continued to feature Megawati and her daughter Puan Maharani, rather than Widodo.[10] Widodo's communication style — contrasting with the old-style, haughty approach of *pejabatism* — and the public's identification of him with social safety net policies[11] (although they were not his ideas) had won him his popularity.[12]

Aburizal Bakrie's campaign strategy for Golkar based itself on the assumption that there was a growing nostalgia for the Suharto era. He repeatedly emphasized this, and also promoted and mobilized some of Suharto's children in his campaign. "It was better in my time, wasn't it?" was a common refrain, referring to a sticker that can be seen here and there on cars, where these words are seen to be coming from Suharto. (This was countered by another sticker with the same words but a picture of Suharto strangling somebody.)

GERINDRA built itself around former Lieutenant-General Prabowo Subianto, whom it has packaged as a military leader. Prabowo appeared at many rallies wearing a *keris* (Javanese and Malay symbol of the *ksatria* or warrior) in his belt. At the rally launching his campaign, he rode in on a horse, *keris* in waist, and surrounded by men dressed in traditional dress, lined up in a very martial manner. Since the last elections in 2009, his supporters have played up his image as "tegas" (firm) in contrast to current President Yudhoyono's image as vacillating, hesitant and slow to act. However, packaging him this way did, at the same time, remind another constituency that Prabowo was dismissed from the Army after 1998 for actions such as the kidnapping of democratic activists and instigating violence.[13] In some ways, GERINDRA offers the only difference which goes beyond style — a shift to militarist governance.

PDI-P and GERINDRA's campaigns succeeded in increasing their vote shares compared to 2009, but neither came near their targets of 27 per cent and 20 per cent respectively. Golkar's campaign did not gain it any increase in votes at all.

There was no serious discussion of vision, direction for the country, or central policy questions. The intense discussion for months up to the elections was only which candidates had "*elektabilitas*" (electability). "*Elektabilitas*" took on an existence of its own, based purely on opinion polls. Campaign rhetoric and advertising assumed grossly vague and abstract forms. All parties had manifestos and policy materials on their websites, but it was not the real "content" of their campaigns.[14] Each, in general, was selling a different style; but we should note that in Prabowo's case, his militarist style has implications for democratic governance.

Their emphasis on style is underpinned by a shared outlook on the basic issues of Indonesian socio-economic development. *No party profiled during the campaign any proposals to seriously move away from the basic parameters of current policies.* This shared outlook also underpins the ease with which all of the parties have been able to announce after the elections that they are willing and able to coalesce with any other party. GOLKAR, GERINDRA and PDI-P will not be in the same coalition to nominate presidential candidates — as they each have their own. But they all have said they wished to work together in the parliament, as have the Islamic parties. Final coalition formations will be decided by power-sharing deals, no matter what the party leaders' rhetoric.

No party can expect to win while telling the Indonesian public — made up of 180 million voters most of whom are poor and have no job security — that they plan no real change in direction, just some minor adjustments here and there. Their emphasis must be where there may be real differences — styles of communication and governance.

This is an insufficient basis for overcoming the public's alienation and inspiring participation. Such a lack of leadership has meant the lack of a sense of central campaigning and has encouraged chaotic, and often contradictory, campaigning at the local level. This can present an image of a mass of self-interested individuals with few ideas for real change. The PDI-P's campaign in particular was often characterized by political chaos at the local level, even to the extent of PDI-P candidates seeing others on their own party list as their main competitors. Widodo had no impact on this state of affairs.

PRESIDENTIAL ELECTIONS, JULY 2014

The PDI-P has now established an agreement with Nasional Demokrat to jointly nominate Widodo. At the time of writing, neither GOLKAR nor GERINDRA has yet announced a coalition that can nominate either Bakrie or Prabowo. The horse-trading continues.

It is important at this point to address a question that is expressed in an often quoted slogan by some campaigners for Widodo: "PDI-P No! Jokowi Yes!" That is, to what extent is there a separation in *some* voters' minds between Widodo and the PDI-P? There is little doubt that such a separation exists. During 2013 and into 2014, all opinion polls showed Widodo scoring higher than the PDI-P. Exit polls on 9 April indicated that significant percentages of voters for all the parties, except GERINDRA and GOLKAR, said they would vote for Widodo in the presidential election. The polling group, *Indikator*, conducted exit polls that showed a 44 per cent support rate for Widodo as against 25 per cent for Prabowo.[15] What explains this?

At one level, this is another manifestation of the extensive popular alienation with all the parties. The more all the political parties are distrusted and disliked, the more political parties *per se* are rejected. As this sentiment deepens, peoples' hopes settle on individuals and not institutions. But their hope is skeptical. One researcher with long experience in Jakarta's urban poor areas, Roanne Van Voorst, captured the ambivalence in a recent article on her dialogue with people she had been observing over a long time:

> He [Jokowi] won't stick to these promises, added my respondents hastily, and that, they said, is not the point... Jokowi is a politician and politicians do such things all the time. And Abdul explained to me that "even though he has good intentions, he will still cooperate with other politicians, so eventually he cannot do what he promises".[16]

This widespread sentiment flows primarily from Widodo's practice of regular visits, known as *blusukan* — as brief and symbolic as they may be — to *kampung* (urban hamlet) communities. This is more important than his actual record, which some researchers have thrown doubts on. The "pro-people" stance of Jakarta governors has often been measured based on their record of evictions of poor people from their communities. Researcher Ian Wilson, with a long experience of Jakarta urban poor communities, writes:

> According to the Jakarta Residents Forum (FAKTA) over 19,000 people were evicted by the administration in 2013. Less than 40 per cent were

offered alternative accommodation, in the form of rental apartments often far from places of work and school.[17]

As the quote from Van Voorst's article shows, the respondents know that Widodo will disappoint them, but they still hope.

The question is whether this kind of hope will be sufficient by itself to ensure Widodo's victory in the face of what will be intensified campaigns by both Prabowo and Bakrie. With his current popularity level, Widodo is clearly "ahead in the race" at the moment. However, the PDI-P's low vote on 9 April indicates that things can go wrong.

Perhaps his "populist" style of communication and the hope that it inspires will be enough. There is not much more he can do to strengthen his image in this particular respect — apart from responding to the attacks of his opponents over the coming ten weeks.[18]

Is there anything more he and the PDI-P can do? The problem is that they, like all the parties, do not have a radically different program from what has gone before them. They are offering the same but with different rhetoric, perhaps "done better" and communicated in a more grassroots friendly style. Will this be enough to mobilize their chaotic political machine — especially with so many now disappointed and indebted candidates — to campaign effectively for them? The other machines, especially Prabowo's, will mobilize and spend even more money. Can it be enough to inspire the 35–40 per cent who has not voted to do so this time? Will the Prabowo militarist style campaign strengthen its emphasis on returning to "firm" (i.e. authoritarian) rule? Will Widodo end his public silence on the issues of Prabowo's past and his approach to governance?[19]

With approximately only 20 per cent of the seats in the parliament, the PDI-P will only make up a third of any majority coalition it is a part of, threatening also the prospect of stable coalitions. The other two-thirds will be made up mostly of parties in the present governing coalition. So, will the PDI-P and Widodo consider how any new campaign and policy approach will be viewed by these parties? Or will they defy them and do something different hoping to win such a big vote for Widodo in July that they can insist on getting their way later.

Nothing is impossible in politics, but there are no signs of such a dramatic turn at the moment.

Notes

1. <http://www.iberita.com/25005/hasil-quick-count-pemilu-lsi-menyatakan-angka-golput-kalahkan-perolehan-suara-pdip>. The 34 per cent figure appears to be a consensus so far among commentators.
2. While no doubt small in number a new phenomenon has been people writing political slogans on their ballot papers. Some of these have appeared in the social media with voters using their mobile phones to photograph them, or other people photographing them when they are held up for the public to see in the counting process. Slogans have included: "Betrayers all of them", and "People representatives, or conglomerates representatives". One photograph was widely circulated with election officials holding up a ballot paper with a big hammer and sickle drawn on it.
3. On the shallowness of Widodo's populism, see Max Lane, "Who will be Indonesian President in 2014?", *ISEAS Perspective*, 18 July 2013.
4. "Daftar Persentase Pemilih Dalam Beberapa Pilkada Terakhir di Indonesia" <http://www.rumahpemilu.org/in/read/2186/Daftar-Persentase-Pemilih-Dalam-Beberapa-Pilkada-Terakhir-di-Indonesia>.
5. See <http://www.indikator.co.id/uploads/20130723190925.23_Juli_2013_Rilis_INDIKATOR.pdf>.
6. For the Quick Count results currently available, see <http://indonesiasatu.kompas.com/quickcount>.
7. For a useful survey of the all the parties see Ulla Fionna and Alexander Arifianto, "Getting to know the Contestants of the 2014 Indonesian Parliamentary Elections", *ISEAS Perspective*, 10 March 2014 <http://www.iseas.edu.sg/documents/publication/ISEAS_Perspective_2014_14-Contestants_2014_Indonesian_Parliamen-tary_Elections.pdf>.
8. <http://www.straitstimes.com/news/asia/south-east-asia/story/jokowi-confident-big-win-pdi-p-indonesias-parli-mentary-polls-2014040>.
9. <http://www.tribunnews.com/nasional/2014/03/31/pencapresan-jokowi-angkat-pdi-perjuangan-melampaui-25-persen-suara>.
10. Rumours are rife that Puan Maharani and Widodo do not get on. Tensions between Puan and Widodo may be undermining the PDI-P's campaigning and politicking efforts.
11. The social safety net policies in Indonesia (health, education, cash hand-outs) originate from the Washington Consensus and have been implemented alongside major cuts in subsidies to fuel, basic consumer commodities and agricultural inputs (fertilizers, etc.).

12. On *pejabatism*, see Max Lane, "Who will be Indonesian President in 2014?", *ISEAS Perspective*, 18 July 2013.
13. An interview with General Wiranto, Prabowo's immediate commander in 1998, has been widely circulated on the internet during the campaign. During the interview Wiranto was asked about Prabowo's dismissal from the armed forces and whether it was proved that he had been involved in kidnappings, Wiranto replied: "Of course, otherwise he would not have been dismissed [from the army]." <http://news.okezone.com/read/2013/01/18/62/748188/wiranto-prabowo-dipecat-dari-militer-karena-penculikan>.
14. On what Joko Widodo "stands for", see John McBeth, "Indonesian Elections: Jokowi's Policy Stance a Mystery" <http://www.asianewsnet.net/INDONESIA-ELECTIONS-Jokowis-policy-stance-a-myster-58612.html>.
15. <http://penaone.com/2014/04/09/jokowi-menang-telak-atas-prabowo/>.
16. <http://asiapacific.anu.edu.au/newmandala/2014/04/16/hope-cynicism-and-jokowi-in-a-jakarta-slum/>.
17. <http://www.thejakartapost.com/news/2014/02/08/floods-housing-security-and-rights-jakarta-s-poor.html>.
18. For example, a group of Jakarta residents, calling themselves JAKARTA BARU, are now taking Widodo to court in a citizen's suit charging him with breach of promise in that he has betrayed his pledge to serve a full five-year term as Governor of Jakarta. The chief lawyer for the group is a candidate for GERINDRA. Widodo has a high profile team of lawyers also representing him <http://us.metro.news.viva.co.id/news/read/488851-tim-jakarta-baru-akan-gugat-jokowi-ke-pengadilan>.
19. It has been people outside the PDI-P, in the NGOs and among the intelligentsia and activists, who are calling for a vote for Widodo as a means of blocking the return of militarist rule. The small radical Left has been campaigning against Prabowo but backing the GOLPUT sentiment and calling in progressives to form a new party.

10

THE ISLAMIC FACTOR IN THE 2014 INDONESIAN ELECTIONS

Gwenael Njoto-Feillard

INTRODUCTION

One of the main surprises from the recently held legislative elections in Indonesia (9 April 2014) was the better-than-expected performance of Islamic parties.[1] Taken together, they managed to garner around 32 per cent of the vote share (as against close to 29 per cent in 2009).[2] Multiple polling institutions had announced for some time that such parties were going to fare poorly. The Prosperous Justice Party (Partai Keadilan Sejahtera, PKS) had been embroiled in a beef graft import scandal in 2013, while the botched experiment of Islamism in the Middle East, following the 2011 Arab Spring uprisings, did not signal anything positive for the advancement of political Islam in Indonesia. However, PKS managed to limit the damage (winning around 6.9 per cent of the votes, down from 7.88 per cent in 2009) by interpreting the graft scandal as a conspiracy

Gwenael Njoto-Feillard is Visiting Fellow at ISEAS. This article was first published on 9 May 2014 as *ISEAS Perspective* 2014/29.

against the party and by relying on its long-term charity strategy on the local level, a common feature of Islamist movements.[3] For sympathizers, whatever happened in Jakarta could not nullify the dedication of PKS cadres in helping communities in dire times, such as the 2013 Jakarta floods or the eruption of Sinabung volcano in 2014. The other important surprise was the National Awakening Party's (Partai Kebangkitan Bangsa, PKB) success in recovering its constituency within the traditionalist organization Nahdlatul Ulama (NU), garnering about 9 per cent of the vote. The United Development Party (Partai Persatuan Pembangunan, PPP — 6.7 per cent) and the National Mandate Party (Partai Amanat Nasional, PAN — 7.5 per cent) have similarly managed to establish themselves as mid-sized parties, whose support will be key to the "big three": PDI-P, Golkar and Gerindra. The Crescent and Star Party (Partai Bulan Bintang, PBB — 1.6 per cent), the only true conservative Islamist party, did not manage to pass the electoral threshold of 3.5 per cent.

With July's presidential elections looming, have the results of the legislative elections shown that political Islam is still a force to be reckoned with? While the current volatility of political manoeuvring makes predictions on future coalitions rather risky, past events may give us hints of things to come.

AN ALLIANCE OF ISLAMIC PARTIES?

One could ask whether the 32 per cent vote share can translate into some form of unity for the coming presidential elections. After all, an alliance of all Islamic parties has been repeatedly called for by some major figures of Indonesian Islam. Among them is PAN's Amien Rais, who was at the helm of the 1999 "Central Axis" (Poros Tengah) that brought Abdurrahman Wahid to power, in a shared dislike of Megawati Soekarnoputri. While Amien Rais now has declared himself favourable to a new alliance, he has also admitted that significant obstacles remain.[4] First, there is no popular figure in sight who can unite Indonesia's Islamic parties. Second, a united stance seems difficult to achieve even within the Islamic parties themselves.[5] The clearest example of this problem is the recent internal rift in the PPP following the official support of its chairman, Suryadharma Ali (SDA), for Prabowo's candidacy. To avoid a major rift within the party, a national meeting cancelled all previous decisions, including SDA's support for Prabowo.[6]

Besides Amien Rais, one of the most vocal figures in favour of the creation of an Islamic coalition has been Din Syamsuddin, head of the reformist organization Muhammadiyah and of the Council of Indonesian Ulamas (MUI, Majelis Ulama Indonesia). On 21 April, around thirty Islamic organizations gathered at MUI's headquarters in Jakarta to declare their support for an alliance.[7] For some time now, MUI has been strategizing to re-establish its authority and present itself as "the true defender of the Islamic *ummah*",[8] it was no surprise to see the organization at the forefront of the initiative.[9] As for Din Syamsuddin's eagerness to see a unitary front of Islamic parties, it seems to be motivated more by his position in MUI or his personal political views than by an official positioning of his organization, Muhammadiyah, which historically has avoided too direct an involvement in national politics.[10]

Realizing that an "Islamic alliance" without the now largest Islamic party, the National Awakening Party (PKB), would leave the initiative rather ineffective, Din Syamsuddin has proposed that the PKB take the helm of the possible alliance. However, the PKB leadership has so far shown no interest in taking such a role or even to support the initiative. Besides the fact that the PKB has probably more to gain in joining relatively secure political alliances (notably with PDI-P), it seems its leaders are wary of an Islamic front that would be in a position to challenge the Indonesian secularist model. NU Chairman Said Aqil Siraj argues that "*the question of religion and the State has been settled in Indonesia in contradistinction with the Middle East*", and the "*dichotomy between Islamic and nationalist parties*" is thus over and should not be revived.[11] The memory of various rifts involving Islamic parties — starting in the early 1950s (Masyumi), then in the 1980s (PPP), and then the ouster of President Abdurrahman Wahid in 2001 — could also be in the minds of the NU leaders.[12]

Moreover, the failed Islamist experiment in the Middle East following the uprisings in 2011 and the violence that ensued also seem to have persuaded the NU/PKB leadership that Indonesia's tolerant model needs to be upheld. In a campaign video, featuring Indonesian-Chinese entrepreneur Rusdi Kirana[13] promoting religious harmony in Indonesia, Said Aqil Siraj declared: "We are not like the Middle East or South Asia. We, the Nahdlatul Ulama, have been the foundation of a Nation that is more tolerant and peaceful".[14] In the background, video extracts of fighting in Syria were being shown.

It is also noteworthy that the Nahdlatul Ulama has complained of being confronted with tactics of infiltration from other organizations, such as the moderate Islamist party PKS or the trans-national movement Hizbut Tahrir Indonesia. Now clearly conscious of the problem, NU circles have adopted an anti-Wahhabi strategy and more generally an anti-radical Islam discourse.[15] Today, these ideological schisms pose an additional obstacle to the formation of a united and sustainable front of Islamic parties.

If one is to read the most recent declarations of their leaders, the PDI-P and the PKB seem close to officially announcing their alliance. It remains to be seen whether the local power base of NU, i.e. the *kyais* (religious leaders of Islamic boarding schools or *pesantren*), will throw their support behind Jokowi. Much depends on the choice of his vice-presidential candidate. Some *kyais* could be susceptible to the claims of Jokowi detractors that have been constantly presenting the Jakarta governor as not being a good Muslim, sometimes even a Christian or, at best, a nominal Muslim (*abangan*). This is probably why the PDI-P has been careful to give an important Islamic dimension to Jokowi's campaign (visiting the *kyais*, the tombs of Muslim saints, etc.) and considers Jusuf Kalla, who is known to be a pious Muslim, a possible vice-presidential candidate.

THE "ANTI-JOKOWI EFFECT"

For the moment, the strategy of Gerindra has been to present Jokowi as a candidate with no track-record and a mere puppet within the PDI-P. The PDI-P itself has been portrayed by Gerindra as being untrustworthy, referring to the Batu Tulis agreement of 2009, where Megawati supposedly promised to endorse Prabowo in 2014 in return for his support as her vice-presidential candidate. Presenting Jokowi as a mere nominal Muslim (*abangan*) and the PDI-P as being on the left of the political spectrum can sway more votes in favour of Prabowo, especially in rural Java, where the *kyais* seem to be more receptive to this kind of discourse and may see Prabowo's militaristic past in a rather positive light.[16] This type of strategy may backfire, though, since a confrontational approach is generally not favoured by the Indonesian public.

However, among the more conservative elements of Indonesian Islam, this type of antagonistic discourse towards Jokowi and the PDI-P has been widespread for quite some time. All currents seem to unite in their opposition to Jokowi's possible presidency. In the words of K.H. Kholil Ridwan, one of MUI's leaders, Jokowi is "not a real Muslim" and permits non-Muslims (Christians) to govern Muslims,[17] which for him means that an "anything-but-Jokowi" strategy is needed in the run-up to the presidential elections.[18] Indeed, the PDI-P candidate has been accused of multiple misdeeds by various currents of conservative Islam, such as being financed by Indonesian- Chinese conglomerates (notably James Riady, CEO of the Lippo Group), Christian missionaries, freemasons and the Rotary Club.[19] Jokowi's recent meeting with foreign ambassadors, at the initiative of Indonesian-Chinese entrepreneur Jacob Soetoyo's,[20] was seen as proof that the PDI-P candidate was amenable to foreign interests, especially those of the United States.[21] It is notable that this type of wild propaganda can strike a chord in some circles and not only in radical ones. A flurry of text messages with such contents have been circulating for quite some time, even in Muslim circles which would be considered "moderate".

The question remains whether Jokowi's rivals will take advantage of this already established and active opposition front. In the mid-1990s, Prabowo Subianto was known to have links with ultra-conservative elements of Indonesian Islam.[22] He had approached DDII (Indonesian Council of Proselytisation) and KISDI (Indonesian Committee for Solidarity with the Islamic World) for support of President Soeharto in 1996. While Prabowo has recently shown a relative readiness to take into account the voices of the more radical elements of Indonesian Islam such as the FPI,[23] he has also been keen on reassuring the Christians/Indonesian-Chinese community of his noble and peaceful intentions. His brother and financier, Hashim Djojohadikusumo, a Christian, has also been presenting Prabowo as the guarantor of ethnic and religious harmony in Indonesia.[24] Thus, it is difficult to know for the moment whether the Gerindra candidate would consider the pro-ultra-conservative strategy to be fruitful or whether he even shares the radicals' ideological orientations. What is clear however is that the latter are rooting for him against Jokowi and the PDI-P, seen as the enemies of Islamic interests.

Some Indonesian scholars have already voiced their concern over the possible religious agenda of Gerindra in attracting conservative forces.[25] Airlangga Pribadi, of Airlangga University in Surabaya, noted that Gerindra's manifesto includes ambiguous principles that risk endangering the secular foundation of the Indonesian State, as the party declared that one of the tasks of the State is to *"guarantee the purity of religious teachings that are recognized by the State (and protect this purity) from deviations and contempt from other religious teachings"*.[26] Similarly, Najib Burhani, a researcher at Indonesia's National Institute of Sciences (LIPI), warned that the presidency of Prabowo could pose a threat to religious pluralism in Indonesia.[27]

CONCLUDING REMARKS

Islam is surely not the only factor having sway in the elections, but it is an important one. The two largest Islamic organizations in Indonesia, the Nahdlatul Ulama and the Muhammadiyah, have historically occupied socio-religious space in such a way that they have posed an obstacle to the growth of conservative forms of Islam from the Middle East.[28] Here again, they will play significant roles, especially in the case of Nahdlatul Ulama, which is courted by both the PDI-P and Gerindra.

Coalition building, however, sometimes overshadows the fact that Indonesian voters will not necessarily follow their parties' choice in the presidential race or respond positively to tactics based on religious persuasions. Quite paradoxically, and as has been happening in other parts of the Muslim World, by entering the political and economic spheres,[29] religion has been secularized and, in a way, desacralized. The elections in July will show how far this is the case, making their results an important marker in the fluctuating relation between religion and the State in this Muslim-majority country.

Notes

1. For an analysis of the preliminary results of the legislative election (based on the quick count method), see Alexander Arifianto, "Unpacking the Results of the 2014 Indonesian Legislative Election", *ISEAS Perspective*, no. 24, 17 April 2014; see also Max Lane, "Indonesia's 2014 Legislative Elections: The Dilemmas of 'Elektabilitas' Politics", *ISEAS Perspective*, no. 25, 23 April 2014.

2. Vote results quoted in this document are the quick count results from the Cyrus-CSIS institutes (www.detik.com).

3. Various interviews with PKS members and sympathizers at Gelora Bung Karno campaign meeting in Jakarta, March 2014.

4. In the meantime, he has declared that he was personally supporting Prabowo Subianto, as Gerindra's candidate was the only one who could "protect" Indonesia from foreign economic interests (quoted are the World Bank, the IMF and the WTO) <http://pemilu.tempo.co/read/news/2014/04/27/270573529/ Puja-puji-Amien-Rais-Buat-Prabowo>.

5. Interview with Bahtiar Effendy, Jakarta, 20 March 2014 and Interview with Andar Nubowo, Jakarta, 20 March 2014.

6. In 2009, PPP had already experienced such an incident, supporting Prabowo, then retracting its support.

7. <http://www.antaranews.com/berita/431324/din-syamsuddin-poros-islam-sulit-terwujud>.

8. Moch Nur Ichwan, "Towards a Puritanical Moderate Islam: The Majelis Ulama Indonesia and the Politics of Religious Orthodoxy", in *Contemporary Developments in Indonesian Islam: Explaining the Conservative Turn*, edited by Martin van Bruinessen (Singapore: Institute of Southeast Asian Studies, 2013).

9. MUI was created in 1971 as a semi-governmental organization by the New Order regime to give further religious justification to its policies. MUI's main purpose was to issue "judicial advices" (fatwa) in Islamic jurisprudence. However, since the fall of the New Order, it has taken a more central role in the religious, but also political and economic fields. MUI is in charge of the highly lucrative sector of halal certification.

10. Eunsook Jung, "Islamic Organizations and Electoral Politics: The Case of Muhammadiyah", *Southeast Asia Research* 22, no. 1 (2014): 73–86.

11. <http://www.muslimedianews.com/2014/04/islam-tidak-perlu-diformalkan-tapi.html?m=1>.

12. The NU became a separate political party in 1952, leaving the Masyumi after a rift concerning mostly the post of Minister of Religious Affairs which Reformists and Traditionalists were competing for. In the early 1980s, the NU decided to leave the Islamic political party PPP after continued conflicts with other groups within the party. In 2001, Abdurrahman Wahid was ousted as President of Indonesia after a move by Amien Rais to convene the MPR to unseat him, this only two years after making him his choice as President against competitor Megawati Soekarnoputri. The NU kyais often relate these events as moments when they were used and then belittled systematically by other Muslim politicians.

13. Rusdi Kirana, founder of Lion Air, Indonesia's fastest growing airline, joined the PKB as deputy-chairman in January 2104 and has been financing the party's campaign since then. For more details, see Greg Fealy, "The Lion of PKB: Rusdi Kirana", 31 March 2014 <http://asiapacific.anu.edu.au/ newmandala/2014/03/31/the-lion-of-pkb-rusdi-kirana/>.

14. <http://www.youtube.com/watch?v=LyU0SI3fzJo&feature=youtube_gdata_ player>.

15. The idea that a puritanical form of Islam coming from the Middle East poses a threat to traditionalist Islam was present at different moments of Indonesian history. This was the case during the early twentieth century evidently, when NU was formed to defend against Reformism. The religious revival of the 1990s was another key moment. For more details on this subject, see Martin van Bruinessen, "Ghazwul fikri or Arabisation? Indonesian Muslim responses to globalisation", in *Dynamics of Southeast Asian Muslims in the era of globalization*, edited by Ken Miichi and Omar Farouk (Tokyo: Japan International Cooperation Agency Research Institute (JICA-RI), 2013), pp. 47–70. For the recent conceptualization of a form of Indonesian "moderate Islam" in opposition to foreign "radical Islam", see <http://www.muslimedianews.com/2014/03/ allahu-akbar-konferensi-ulama-keluarkan.html?m=1>.

16. It is noteworthy as well that in the early 2000s, collaborators of Prabowo were courting the rural *pesantren* milieu and peasants association in Java through the fertilizing business. Personal observations from a field-trip in Sunan Drajat Pesantren in East-Java in 2003.

17. Here, he is referring to the fact that Jokowi's deputy-governor of the Greater Jakarta Province is Basuki Tjahaja Purnama ("Ahok"), an Indonesian Chinese and practising Protestant. If Jokowi gets elected president of the Republic, Ahok will become in effect the governor of Jakarta, a possibility that the conservatives clearly dread. Another case is the one of Susan Jasmine Zulfikri, a Catholic and local civil servant (*lurah*), whose administrative authority on Muslims has been challenged by the FPI.

18. <http://www.voa-islam.com/read/indonesiana/2014/04/13/29841/ketua-mui-kiai-kholil-ridwan-karena-jokowi-jakarta-akan-jatuh-ke-ahok/#sthash. o9qfrjyl.6OALMf9r.dpbs>.

19. <http://www.voa-islam.com/read/indonesiana/2014/04/11/29826/inilah-dosa-mega-dan-jokowi/#sthash.rcLE-m2A9.eIvxQDhN.dpbs>.

20. Jacob Seotoyo is president director and commissioner for a number of companies under the umbrella of the Gesit Group. One of these companies is PT. Gesit Sarana Perkasa, the owner of the luxury hotel project "JS Luwansa" in Kuningan, South Jakarta <http://news.detik.com/read/2014/04/15/025239/2555134/ 10/siapa-jacob-soetoyo-yang-pertemukan-jokowi-mega-dan-dubes-asing>.

21. <http://hizbut-tahrir.or.id/2014/04/15/jokowi-bertemu-dubes-asing-kedaulatan-indonesia-terancam/>; <http://www.republika.co.id/berita/pemilu/menuju-ri-1/14/04/16/n42kvy-temui-wakil-vatikan-jokowi-disebut-serahkan-leher-ke-asing>.

22. Robert W. Hefner, *Civil Islam: Muslims and Democratization in Indonesia* (Princeton, NJ: Princeton University Press, 2000), p. 201.

23. <http://suara.com/news/2014/04/16/125856/fpi-ajukan-syarat-sebelum-berikan-dukungan-kepada-prabowo/>.

24. <http://www.thejakartaglobe.com/news/prabowos-brother-gives-sby-f-minus-on-religious-tolerance/>.

25. <http://pemilu.tempo.co/read/news/2014/04/27/270573645/Berbagai-Ketakutan-jika-Prabowo-Jadi-Presiden>.

26. "Menjamin kemurnian ajaran agama yang diakui oleh negara dari segala bentuk penistaan dan penyelewengan dari ajaran agama" <http://pemilu.tempo.co/read/news/2014/04/27/270573645/Berbagai-Ketakutan-jika-Prabowo-Jadi-Presiden>.

27. "Peneliti LIPI: Kaum Minoritas Terancam Jika Prabowo Presiden", tribunnews.com, 25 April 2014 <http://www. tribunnews.com/pemilu-2014/2014/04/25/peneliti-lipi-kaum-minoritas-terancam-jika-prabowo-presiden>.

28. Vedi R. Hadiz, "No Turkish Delight: The Impasse of Islamic Party Politics in Indonesia", *Indonesia*, vol. 92, 2011, pp. 1–18.

29. Greg Fealy and Sally White, *Expressing Islam: Religious Life and Politics in Indonesia*, Indonesia Update Series, Singapore, ISEAS, 2008.

11

VOTE-BUYING IN INDONESIA'S 2014 ELECTIONS
The Other Side of the Coin

Ulla Fionna

INTRODUCTION

Vote-buying in Indonesian elections is certainly nothing new. Since the days of Suharto, *serangan fajar* (dawn attack) — which refers to the effort of bribing voters to vote for a particular party conducted in the early hours on polling day — has continued to play an important role to this day. Since the fall of Suharto's New Order in 1998 however, there are two important trends to note. On the one hand, the predictable effects of vote-buying may have been reduced by greater awareness amongst voters, as they now enjoy the freedom to vote and know they can benefit by taking the bribe and still vote according to their own preference. At the same time,

---

Ulla Fionna is Fellow at ISEAS. This article was first published on 4 June 2014 as *ISEAS Perspective* 2014/35.

parties have quickly realized that vote-buying is expensive and probably not very effective.

In the current electoral system, candidates are at the centre of the voting process. Put simply, candidates largely run and fund their own campaigns, and they face tough competition from those not only from other parties, but also from their own parties, to win seats.[1] As such they have been forced to choose methods they deem most efficient in grabbing votes amongst the electorate to which they are largely unknown. One simple way to do this is to attract votes with material benefits, which has resulted in large-scale vote-buying. The 2014 elections have demonstrated that this phenomenon has evolved to be more extensive, sophisticated, and better organized than before. Indeed, various observations have strongly indicated that, compared to the 2009 elections, the scale and extent of money politics in this year's elections have been remarkable. An independent observer has used the words "massive, vulgar, and brutal" to describe the extent of transactional politics during the elections.[2] The wide-ranging cases that have been reported featured most notably the door-to-door approach, where typically voters would be handed an envelope containing a specific candidate's name and a certain amount of money to persuade them to vote for that particular person.[3] Less-direct and more innovative methods are plenty, including interest-free loans, free blood tests, plant seeds for farmers, insurance for motorbike taxis, and lucky draws offering freezers and even a Hajj trip.[4]

Vote-buying also takes place at different stages of the campaign. Candidates provide gifts as a way to introduce themselves to voters. These could then be followed up by hand-outs at mass rallies, and donations to build or improve community facilities. To ensure that these tactics work, the candidates may then proceed with vote-buying much closer to the polling day.[5] Aside from these methods, this year's election also revealed that vote-buying was done not only by the candidates, but also by organizers and scrutinizers — who were supposed to maintain the integrity of the voting process. A case in point is Gerindra Party's candidate in Pasuruan (East Java), Agustina Amprawati who admitted to bribing thirteen sub-district electoral committees (PPK, Panitia Pemilihan Kecamatan). The committee members were paid a total of Rp117 million (approx. US$10,172) in exchange for 5,000 votes for the candidate in all the sub-districts that the committee was in charge of. Feeling cheated when she still failed to secure a seat, she reported the case to the election watchdog (Panitia Pengawas Pemilihan Umum, Panwaslu).[6]

While vote-buying has been relatively well-documented, there is a different side to the phenomenon that is less known, namely, that of the intermediaries. This article shares some insights from the individuals who buy votes, and/or persuade voters on behalf of the candidates. It shows that there are various nuances in the practice of vote-buying in Indonesia. While the practice is becoming more institutionalized, what has not been stressed enough is that there is demand for vote-buying not only from candidates, but also from voters — primarily from low-income constituents who see the elections as a way to make short-term gains. It will also be demonstrated here, that although the work of the intermediaries largely bends the principles of free elections, ironically they could also increase interest in the elections.

HOW VOTE-BUYING ON THE GROUND WORKS

The 2014 legislative elections have institutionalized the need and demand for field co-ordinators (korlap, acronym for koordinator lapangan). These individuals played a significant role in how people voted on 9 April 2014. Interviews with two of these korlap revealed their side of the practice. They are seasoned practitioners who operate in their local communities.[7] In every legislative election since 1999, they have worked for various candidates to either persuade voters or simply buy votes. Established shortly before the 2009 elections, the current electoral system abolished the party ranking list, thus allowing every candidate an equal chance to be elected.[8] This created and strengthened the demand for the korlap profession as candidates' success now depends on the direct votes they garner.[9] Each of the two korlap interviewed worked for two separate candidates during the 2009 and 2014 elections.

Although it would be easy to assume that money is their only motivation, and that they would have no allegiance to a specific party, there are specific nuances to this aspect. The two korlap are friends, but often worked for different parties. This is the case because, while korlap A has chosen to work exclusively for Partai Demokrat (Democratic Party, PD), korlap B decided to work for any candidate but PD's — based on a particularly bad previous experience. Thus, party allegiance or non-allegiance can be a strong determinant of their decision to work for particular candidate(s).

In addition, *korlap* B noted that he always investigates the candidates that he works for. Specifically, other than choosing candidates that are not from Partai Demokrat, he would find out the background and credentials of the candidate(s). He would look for evidence that the candidate(s) have worked in and/or for the community, and not just rich individuals with money to spend. He mentioned that if the candidate had worked in local community organizations such as Karang Taruna (a typical small-scaled local youth organization), or was involved in some social work — he would be more willing to assist him/her. However, he would not rule out a "newcomer". He would talk to the candidate to gauge what his/her interests truly are, what his/her programmes would be, and whether in general the candidate is trustworthy. The *korlap* also follows trends of electability and see which candidates have populist programmes, as electability and populist programmes would make their chosen candidates even easier to sell. If he, by the end of his investigations still does not feel confidence in the candidate, he claimed that he would not proceed in his service.

Because of the friendship between the two *korlap*, they would coordinate with each other to ensure that they would not intrude onto each other's turf. For instance, if one has worked on a particular RT/RW,[10] the other would stay away from it. If both feel strongly about working in a particular one, they may also negotiate to decide how they would divide the constituents that they could target. Beyond negotiating however, the way they operate also reveals the level of management that they need to possess to succeed in their work.

Their job requires in-depth knowledge of the people in their community. For them, this is relatively easy as they have lived there all their lives. Such knowledge is important for identifying potential voters whom they can persuade or buy. Because they know the individuals quite well, it is easy for them to choose their targets — which are usually swing- and first-time voters. It is considered risky and unproductive to approach supporters of other parties. Quite logically, they also would not approach voters whom they think would already vote for candidates they were working for.

Interestingly, they stressed that it is not always about money. *Korlap* B revealed that he had different methods to persuade would-be voters. He would first try talking to them. He would ask whether he/she would vote, and gauge who the likely candidate of choice is. Afterwards he would try to "sell" his candidate. For him, this is easy to do as he genuinely supports the particular candidate(s). His approach is to convince the voters to think about what is best for his community — or ask whether the party/candidate that they had voted for in the previous election had really worked to improve the community. In urging voters to think this way, he aims to convince them to vote for his candidate instead. Stressing further that it is less about money, the *korlap* mentioned that they care about their pride. After working across a number of elections for a variety of candidates, these *korlap* cannot afford to lose face. This priority entails keeping their reputation intact by ensuring both success rate in helping candidates, and maintaining a good relationship with the community. Pride is also the reason cited when they claimed that they do not specify any tariff for their service.

When money does play a part, the *korlap* claim that it is often the voters who approach them asking "How come you are not giving away money?" (In Javanese: "*Sampeyan kok gak bagi-bagi duik?*"). Such a question indicates that the community knows and accepts what they do. The question also indicates a growing perception among voters that elections provide an opportunity to make easy money. This can be understood in the context of the poverty in these communities, and that voters are desperate for some kind of tangible benefits from the elections. This further fuels the demand for the *korlap*'s work. Also, demand can come from the candidates themselves, who sometimes have specific ideas of how many votes they need/want from specific polling stations, and ask the *korlap* to help them to secure the votes.

Once approached by voters, the *korlap* would know that for these voters it is indeed about money. What they would do then was to collect identity cards from them, typically by asking them how many people they have in their households, and then give them the name of the candidate that they need to vote for to get the money. In these cases, the approach is quite straightforward. The voters get 50 per cent of the money[11] prior to voting and 50 per cent after — once the votes are tallied at the local voting booth and the *korlap* are convinced the voters have voted as they were supposed to.

In other cases, where they see potential voters gathered as a particular group, such as the local Qur'anic study group (*pengajian*) or local football club, they would make a direct approach and ask them what they need. Typically the answers would be new Qur'an, equipment for praying, or new uniform. The down payment system is applicable in these instances too, where the voters would then be registered, and half of what they need would be provided before polling day, and the other half after — once the votes from them are realized as agreed. It should be noted here that although *korlap* B claims that he never uses intimidation, *korlap* A does. What he would do in this instance is to remind the voters that there would be some consequences — often unspecified — if they did not vote for the candidate as they promised.

Due to the nature of the work requiring them to deal with candidates as well as voters and the election watchdog; understandably there are risks that the *korlap* bear. Essentially, they are the contacts that connect voters to the candidates. This means that if anything goes wrong it is them that voters would go after. They shared stories of having to use their own money to pay the voters off, in cases where the losing candidates had run away. Other risks come from the election watchdogs, who can report and prosecute them. They claim that these however, are easier to manage, as candidates typically have set aside bribe money for these officers. Their stories suggest how powerful they can be, particularly against the election watchdog — suggesting that reform on the role and accountability of the election watchdog is urgent.

BEYOND MONEY IN MONEY POLITICS

The *korlap*'s work clearly skews the principles of democracy. While ideally voters should make a free choice, which entails that there should largely be no other incentive than choosing representatives they trust to accommodate their needs; in reality, the *korlap* intervenes, somewhat like grassroots activists, except that they have at their disposal money and menace as optional tools of persuasion. The role of *korlap*, as explicated here, gives a more nuanced picture of money politics in Indonesia. In particular, it demonstrates that vote-buying is not simply a matter of demand and supply — it employs mechanics that involve complex social relations and deep local knowledge. Firstly, for efficiency, they target swing and first-time voters — voters who are largely non-partisan. Because of this tendency, they may very well have contributed to the reduction of the number of non-voters, and actually improved electoral turnout. Evidently, the rate of non-voters has gone down, from 29 per cent in 2009 to just under 25 per cent in 2014.[12] Nonetheless, concerns should be raised about the motivation of voters and how rampant money politics has been. As the *korlap* themselves have indicated, in this year's election, practically every political party was engaged in it.

Secondly, for the *korlap* there is a moral discourse intertwined with the economic aspect of their vocation. *Korlap* B suggested that he sought accountability from the candidates. He demanded of every candidate that he had helped to genuinely work for their communities. He claimed that he would check on them every once in a while, to see what kind of contribution they had made. He mentioned a few interesting cases on working for a variety of candidates. One was in which he ended up in confrontation with a candidate who owed money to be paid to the voters who had cast their votes for him. In this case, he ended up having to use his own money to pay voters. Failure to pay the voters, he said, would have cost him his profession and pride. If problems arise, a *korlap* would rather confront the candidates, than face the electorate — particularly as the areas they work in are also where they live, so they need to maintain congenial relationships with the locals. He also voiced strong displeasure towards those whom he had helped but had done very little for the community afterwards.

CONCLUDING REMARKS

Undoubtedly, there are flaws in Indonesian elections. The narrative here clearly points to one: that the elections enable the profession of vote-buyers to flourish. The fact that every candidate ran his/her campaign independently has further strengthened this profession. After all, candidates seem to be convinced that it is impossible to be elected without distributing money. However, this article has shown vote-buying to be a process embedded in complex social relations and contexts. To ensure the durability of their vocation and their social standing in their respective communities, *korlap* are incentivized to select electable candidates to support, and thereafter to check on their accountability.

While we cannot claim that the cases elaborated on here are representative, they do show that in the processes of vote-buying, there are considerations beyond goods and rupiah.

Notes

1. Around 200,000 people stood for election to 20,257 seats in the Regional and Provincial Legislative Councils (DPRD), the House of Representatives (DPR) and the Regional Representatives Council (DPD). Of these, 6,607 candidates from twelve parties competed for the 560 seats in the DPR, while the remainder ran for the 132 seats in the DPD, the 2,137 provincial seats and the 17,560 regional seats. There are 1,344 new seats, mostly in the regional parliaments and 123 in provincial parliaments. See Max Lane, "Indonesia's 2014 Legislative Elections: The Dilemmas of 'Elektabilitas' Politics", *ISEAS Perspective*, 23 April 2014 <http://www.iseas.edu.sg/documents/publication/ISEAS_Perspective_2014_25-The-Dilemmas-of-'Elektabilitas'-Politics.pdf>.

2. "Pemantau Pemilu: Politik Uang Kali Ini Sangat Masif, Vulgar dan Brutal" [Election Observer: Money Politics This Time Around is Massive, Vulgar, and Brutal], *Kompas*, 21 April 2014 <http://nasional.kompas.com/read/2014/04/21/2000277/Pemantau.Pemilu.Politik.Uang.Kali.Ini.Sangat.Masif.Vulgar.dan.Brutal> (accessed 29 April 2014).

3. See, for example, Erwin Daryanto, "Begini Praktik Politik Uang Terjadi di Pileg 2014", detiknews, 24 April 2014 <http://news.detik.com/pemilu2014/read/2014/04/24/060747/2563849/1562/begini-praktik-poli-tik-uang-terjadi-di-pileg-2014>, "Praktek Politik Uang Pemilu di Lampung Door to Door" [The Practice of Money Politics in Lampung is through Door-to-Door], Tempo.co, 9 April 2014 <http://pemilu.tempo.co/read/news/2014/04/09/269569301/Praktek-Politik-Uang-Pemilu-di-Lampung-Door-to-Door> (both sites accessed 2 June 2014).

4. Novrida Manurung and Neil Chatterjee, "Free Loans Trump Noodles in Indonesia Voter Race", Bloomberg.com, 9 April 2014 <http://www.bloomberg.com/news/2014-04-08/free-loans-trump-noodles-in-indonesia-voter-race-southeast-asia.html> (accessed 2 June 2014).

5. Edward Aspinall, "Money politics: The distribution of money, goods, and other

benefits is an integral part of electioneering in Indonesia", *Inside Indonesia*, Edition 116 (Apr–Jun 2014) <http://www.insideindonesia.org/weekly-articles/money-politics-2> (accessed 2 June 2014).

6. "Sogok Rp117 Juta tapi Gagal, Caleg Cantik ini Merasa Ditipu" [Bribing Rp117 Million but Failed, this Pretty Candidate is Feeling Cheated], *Kompas*, 24 April 2014 <http://indonesiasatu.kompas.com/read/2014/04/24/1026159/Sogok. Rp.117.Juta.tapi.Gagal.Caleg.Cantik.Ini.Merasa.Ditipu> (accessed 2 June 2014).

7. The two men are middlemen or *makelaar* — people come to them when they want to buy or sell houses, land, vehicles and other goods, asking them for their service to find buyers and sellers and they will be paid a percentage of the agreed purchase price.

8. The party ranking is a closed list system, where parties determine the rank of the candidates. The voters cast their votes for the party, but the individual who will occupy the seat is chosen by the parties. Since 2009 with the open system, voters cast their votes directly for the individual candidates, regardless of their rank in the list, so voters choose the candidate and the party.

9. On 23 December 2008, the Indonesian Constitutional Court annulled Article 214 of Law No. 10 of 2008 on Parliamentary Elections to put an end to the party ranking list and let only the number of votes determine a candidate's success at securing a seat.

10. RT/RW are the smallest administration units in Indonesian community. RT stands for Rukun Tetangga (Neighbourhood Association), RW stands for Rukun Warga (Community Association). Rukun Tetangga is a small administration unit consisting around fifteen neighbouring households, and Rukun Warga is a larger administration unit consisting of several (usually around five) RTs.

11. The "average" rate for individual voters in Malang area was around Rp50,000 or around US$4. The government regulates that employers in Malang should pay their employees a minimum of Rp1,587,000 (less than US$137) per month.

12. Dhani Irawan, "Dibanding Tahun 2009, Angka Golput Pemilu 2014 Lebih Rendah", detiknews, 10 May 2014 <http://news.detik.com/pemilu2014/re ad/2014/05/10/074125/2578828/1562/dibanding-tahun-2009-angka-golput-pemilu-2014-lebih-rendah> (accessed 2 June 2014).

12

GAP NARROWS BETWEEN CANDIDATES IN INDONESIAN PRESIDENTIAL ELECTIONS

Max Lane

After an extensive pre-campaign lobbying period to form political coalitions, the presidential election campaigning has been ongoing for three weeks. There have been three nationally televised debates between the two candidates (with each debate focusing on a specific topic) and a nationally televised "dialogue" between the presidential candidates and the Indonesian Chamber of Commerce (KADIN). There has been a flurry of activities as the presidential candidates and their spokespersons immersed themselves in campaigning; billboards and advertising are everywhere.

It has become fairly clear what the division within the Indonesian elite is about. The two candidates, Joko Widodo (from PDI-P) and Prabowo

---

Max Lane is Visiting Senior Fellow at ISEAS, Lecturer in Southeast Asian Politics and History at Victoria University, and Honorary Associate in Indonesian Studies at the University of Sydney. He has been in Indonesia watching the election process. This article was first published on 4 July 2014 as *ISEAS Perspective* 2014/39.

Subianto (from GERINDRA), represent two quite different paths into the future (or back to the past) for Indonesia, but both emerge from within the Indonesian ruling elite. Widodo harks from the new regional elite that blossomed with Indonesia's experiment with decentralization. Prabowo is very much tied to the old elite of the New Order and, while very wealthy in his own right, is also the brother of an extremely wealthy businessman. He is a former son-in-law of Suharto and the son of a former Suharto minister, who is also a wealthy businessman.[1] At the moment, most polls put Widodo between 5 per cent and 7 per cent ahead of Prabowo, with between 20–30 per cent still undecided. Widodo, although still ahead in the polls, appears to have lost the massive lead he had earlier in the year, when some polls had him at 70 per cent.

The "visions" offered by the two candidates reflect the main division within the Indonesian capitalist class. There are the large conglomerates aspiring to restore their crony status, represented by Prabowo and Aburizal Bakrie (Golkar chairman) and there is the ocean of *kabupaten* (regency) and provincial capitalists, represented by Widodo and Jusuf Kalla, who make up the bulk of the elites of local branches of political parties throughout the country.[2] Since 2000, *kabupaten* and provincial capitalists have had more space for intervention in politics as a result of the direct election of regional leaders such as bupatis (regents), mayors and governors and more budgetary power for local parliaments. Widodo himself is an example of this dynamic, having gone from being a central leader of the Solo business community, to mayor of Solo city and then Governor of Jakarta before standing for the Presidency. Prabowo is from a business family that grew wealthy after his father returned to Indonesia following Suharto's seizure of power. Both Prabowo and his brother, Hashim Djojohadikusumo, have grown their businesses as rent-seekers in the natural resources sectors.

In the first presidential debate, Prabowo made a point of criticizing direct elections for bupati and mayors, arguing for a return to the system where regional parliaments chose them. (Actually, in the old system, the regional parliaments only made recommendations to the President, who made the appointments.) Widodo defended the current system as more democratic, but suggested that the local elections be held at the same time throughout the country to save money. Prabowo indicated that he did not approve of the formation of more *kabupaten* administrative units; Widodo supported them if smaller district governments could encourage local business. Prabowo offers — very demagogically and with no detail — promises of big project development to make Indonesia an "Asian Tiger", while Widodo offers more support for small and medium businesses in the field and to cut "red-tape" (the need for permissions) for all businesses (echoing both his background and the current push by neoliberal organizations such as the International Finance Corporation). Prabowo claims that huge amounts of wealth — almost a trillion U.S. dollars — are being funnelled overseas or constitute a lost potential, which he calls huge "leakages" and emphasizes that stopping this leakage is the way to fund the big projects, although he provides no details on how he would stop this. Widodo, however, does not mention the "leakage" of wealth, except with regards to illegal logging and fishing. He defended former President Megawati's earlier sale of the telecommunications company INDOSAT to overseas buyers on the grounds that there was a financial crisis, but said he would buy the shares back. He took a soft line on any need to renegotiate contracts with overseas companies. When pressed by members of the Indonesian Chamber of Commerce on the need for cheaper credit for long-term projects, Widodo responded that he agreed and that more low-interest loans had to be found from overseas.

These different perspectives on economic policy between the *kabupaten* capitalist and the conglomerate capitalist have not attracted a lot of discussion in the mainstream or social media. The public discussion has been more determined by the difference in political perspectives held by the two candidates.

Prabowo's political perspective, as he has elaborated for some time now, is very much a return to Suhartoism, but with more pageantry and demagoguery. He asserts his support for democracy, but for "constructive" and not "destructive" democracy, which he raised again in the first national debate, echoing perhaps Suharto's old term of "Panca Sila Democracy". He is calling for an end to direct elections for bupatis and mayors (although his vice-presidential running mate from a typical locally-based party, the National Mandate Party, contradicted him on this in the first debate). Prabowo's demagoguery constantly attacks all political parties except his own and all politicians in general. His style, with a *keris* (Javanese dagger) stuck in his belt, a Garuda Bird badge on his shirt and pride in his military record, emphasizes his militarism. Prabowo has accepted support from and declared his willingness to work with such organizations as the (notorious) radical Islamic group Front Pembela Islam (Defenders of Islam Front) and the ultra-nationalist Pemuda Pancasila, both semi-militia groups that have acted against human rights and left-wing and religious minorities. He advocates a return to the original 1945 Constitution, which would eliminate many of the liberal democratic-style institutions that have emerged over the last decade.

There is little doubt that this outlook, backed by state power, would be an immediate threat to the expanded democratic space won by the 1990s pro-democracy movement that forced Suharto out of power. It would usher in a period of increasing social and political tension and, probably sooner rather than later, threaten the existence of any democratic space at all. It is this threat against democratic space, and pluralism — space for minorities, especially religious and secular groups — that has galvanized much of the urban, secular, social media-based, big city, lower middle class against Prabowo.

Widodo's perspectives, more by implication than explicit elaboration, promise a continuation of the political status quo. Some of Widodo's supporters point to the emergence of large numbers of volunteer groups and the very impressive Jalan Sehat (Health Walk) mobilization that was turned into a Widodo support rally in Jakarta on 20 June. The photo of Widodo, wearing a simple white T-shirt holding up the two-finger sign — he is candidate number 2 on the ballot — in front of 100,000 people at the National Monument is already becoming iconic. This new "volunteerism", say these supporters, represents a qualitative improvement in democratic life.[3] This is a gross over-estimation of the phenomenon. In a country of 190 million voters, the phenomenon is minuscule (especially given that its duration was short and levels of organization were highly limited beyond "lead-up" demonstrations).

Widodo's "Vision and Mission" document lodged with the Elections Commission (KPU) does explicitly commit to modern human rights norms and to resolving the long series of human rights violations, including the 1965 mass killings as well as the 1998 kidnappings and disappearances, in which Prabowo has been implicated. However, apart from the occasional mention, in passing, reported online, this has not been a campaign theme. Widodo has not taken the opportunity of any of his national television appearances to give a clear public commitment on these issues. Moreover, he has accepted support, in his coalition, from retired military officers whom major human rights institutions also consider to have committed grave violations of human rights, such as General Hendropriyono and Muchdi,[4] whom many consider to be responsible for the murder of human rights activist Munir. Notably, Widodo is not openly fighting Prabowo on these issues himself, making no clear public commitments, and letting supporters outside the party he actually represents make the promises. Occasionally these supporters make promises that he has needed to rebut straightaway, such as the promise by Musdah Muchdi, Director of the Megawati Institute, to abolish the religion category on ID cards.[5]

While Widodo has not taken up the fight with Prabowo on human rights and democratic issues, for that sector of society for whom democratic rights is important, the difference is clear. Whatever deficiencies exist in the status quo, a return to a Suhartoist dictatorship — and a demagogically defended Suhartoism at that — would be a major blow for any kind of democratic progress in the country.

There is no doubt that mass frustration, and even hatred, towards an elite exposed as corrupt, degenerate and "transactional", i.e. obsessed with enriching themselves with deals, frames much of the current political atmosphere.[6] Both Widodo and Prabowo try to respond to this. Widodo offers a "revolusi mental" (mental revolution), where corruption will primarily be fought by example and education — but backed by more funds for the Corruption Eradication Commission as well[7] — which Vice- Presidential candidate Yusuf Kalla promised in the first national debate. Widodo's whole marketing campaign is based on selling himself as "sederhana, jujur dan merakyat" ("simple, honest and close to the people"). The fact that he is not a deal- making conglomerate cum former crony billionaire, but rather "only" a successful millionaire who was a *kabupaten*-level furniture exporter with modest lifestyle habits (as far as we can see), helps him sell this image. What has clinched it for him among his lower-class support base has been his willingness to make frequent local visits to where poor people work and live (although not to factories). Prabowo's response to the corrupt, degenerate and craven elite is to threaten demagogically their sub- jugation — but again he does not name names or specify how this will be done (not surprising given his ultra-elite status).

It is probably in relation to another aspect of the rhetorical war where Prabowo seems to have been able to increase his poll popularity over the last several months. Prabowo has waged a rhetorical *jihad* of sorts against the extent of poverty in Indonesia and has continuously proclaimed that this has been made possible by the huge *"kebocoran"* ("leakage") of wealth from Indonesia to the outside world. He identifies this leakage as the result of foreign ownership and/or domination of Indonesia's natural resources and of contracts and agreements which excessively benefit foreign parties. His rhetoric and emphasis on this is consistent and indeed almost jihad-like, even if he avoids being specific about how he would end this situation. In the national debate on foreign policy and defence, he even asked what the use of having tanks and planes was if the people were in poverty. Widodo's response to the issue of poverty has been much more low-key, flashing his free health and education cards — important symbols of the social safety net that has been built in Indonesia in accordance with the neo-liberal post-Washington consensus, and paid for by abolishing the subsidies that kept down inflation in the past.

So the contrast on this issue of poverty and foreign exploitation is a *tegas* (firm) military man who says he will wage a war against poverty and the extraction of Indonesia's wealth by foreigners, and the former Mayor of Solo offering a social safety net and better management of existing available funds. This contrast may be winning over new support for Prabowo, narrowing Widodo's lead. Widodo supporters, even the significant liberal NGO and intellectual left supporters who are campaigning for him, and a range of commentators, seem to ignore the fact that the picture that Prabowo paints of Indonesian society — even if he does it for demagogic purposes — is more or less accurate. The overwhelming mass of Indonesians are poor, and in terms of 21st century international living standards of income, education, health, culture and leisure that they see existing in the First World through the media, and manifested before their eyes on a daily basis in the rapidly growing and highly westernized Indonesian middle and upper classes, the 150 million or more poor voters are in fact extremely poor and disgracefully left-behind. There is no doubt that there is a widespread, painful resentment of this very real situation among those 150 million.

To ignore the economic and social conditions created by long-term structures of economic dependence and underdevelopment and confine analysis to the immediate issues of rule of law in human rights, corruption and transactional elite politics in understanding Indonesian developments, especially (but not only) in relation to identifying deeper trends, is a major mistake.

Prabowo appeals for support using demagogy, claiming he will wage an all-out fight against poverty and foreign extraction of wealth. In line with the status quo that Yudhoyono has presided over and compatible with the agenda advanced by the World Bank, Widodo offers better technocratic management of existing available funds to provide gradual improvements, with assistance in the immediate term in the form of a social safety net for the urban poor — but while articulating no policies or effective rhetoric for addressing the structural problem of poverty. If the polls are correct, the mass of voters appear close to being evenly divided on who has the more credible answer. There is probably still time for either candidate to come up with new rhetoric or marketing that could drag a few extra percentage points in either direction.

While the two candidates clearly espouse economic and political perspectives that emerge from their class backgrounds — crony capitalist or regional petit bourgeois capitalist — and their political histories — Suharto military power player and regional post-dictatorship, decentralization politician, it would be a mistake to conclude that the broad political and business elite is divided so clearly on these lines. Opportunism — or to use the political scientist's euphemism, transactional politics — has been the obvious motivation behind how the elite is divided, at both national and local levels. There are no doubt plenty of *kabupaten* capitalists in Prabowo's coalition, either as individual supporters or as a part of the party machinery of one of the supporting parties. Widodo's coalition has the open support of conglomerate capitalist Surya Paloh and PDI-P members of parliament have certainly suggested that they have received support from big capital (although there are now criticisms that the money *langsung hilang* — disappears immediately — and is not getting used in the campaign). Without doubt, we will see after the elections many suddenly switch sides or exposed as having supported both sides all along.

The opportunism was on gaudy public display in the period of forming the nominating coalitions. Neither the PDI-P nor GERINDRA had enough votes or seats in parliament to nominate presidential and vice presidential candidates and had to seek partners. During that period *almost* all of the parties at one time or another stated that they could work with either Widodo or Prabowo. The exceptions were the National Democrats, under Paloh, that quickly aligned with PDI-P and Widodo and the Prosperous Justice Party (PKS) that made it clear quickly that they would go with GERINDRA and Prabowo. There were a few weeks of vacillation, even with the big players like GOLKAR smiling and shaking hands in public with both candidates. GOLKAR, headed by a classic ex-crony, Aburizal Bakrie, eventually went with Prabowo.

The wheeling and dealing also saw renegades from almost all parties defying the party line. Once the coalitions were formed, the first activity of both candidates was to seek out as many endorsements as possible from other members of the elite, whether they are local level elite such as pesantren leaders or former and recent national political figures.

This campaign for endorsements also targeted retired senior military officers, which has resulted in the most bitter of mutual incriminations. Retired military figures supporting Widodo — such as former intelligence chief, Hendropriyono, who is himself identified by all the human rights groups as responsible for massacres and other human rights violations, described Prabowo as a psychopath. Return insults have been no less nasty. Finally, as many expected would happen, the document prepared by the Military Honour Council that recommended that Prabowo be "diberhentikan dari keprajuritan" (that his military activity be terminated) i.e. that he be removed from the army, was leaked and widely circulated and discussed in the media. This has further exacerbated the rift between retired officers. Prabowo's former superior, General Wiranto, whose Hanura Party is in Widodo's coalition, held a press conference confirming the veracity of the document. Wiranto had already confirmed several times that the Council had concluded that Prabowo had to be held responsible for the kidnappings of student and other anti-Suharto activists in 1997 and 1998. Wiranto's statement was met with insults from retired officers on the other side, and even a demonstration of former KOPASSUS officers. What is unclear is to what extent this bitter clash is reflected among serving officers. Prabowo is the first truly polarizing political figure for both elite and masses for decades. One factor influencing the impact of this kind of division over Prabowo's past is Suharto's campaign against a critical historical consciousness, which has been very effective in creating uncertainty among the public about what version of history is credible. There is no universally or even widely shared historical memory.[8]

Having decided their alignments, the fight becomes a desperate struggle among the elite to gain or protect positions. This is even true for the leaders of the major labour unions who hope for ministerial positions, with some supporting Widodo and some — including the most active union, the Metal Workers Federation — supporting Prabowo.

For the mass of the poor earning between US$1 and US$5 a day, the choices are hardly inspiring. Both sides have had big and impressive-looking mobilizations but in the context of 190 million voters, they do not indicate a high level of popular active participation. That section of the liberal-minded educated lower and middle layers of the middle class — the social media sector of society — have probably been the most active, forming volunteer brigades, writing songs, filming ads and making jingles for Widodo. But overall, even as opinions crystallize behind one or another candidate assessing who will credibly improve their situation, the mood remains overall passive. In a society where the political culture has been for forty years a patron–client culture, where the mass of the population feels dependent on the ruling elite, the elections are about choosing which patron they feel most comfortable being dependent on.

In the parliamentary elections around 65 million people out of 185 million voters did not vote or voted informally. Most commentators and politicians are sensing that the absentee vote will go down for the presidential election, but the decline may not be as great as expected. The low votes for parties and the high absentee votes reflect the alienation of a significant sector of society from the existing parties. There are a number of activist groups and coalitions — such as the Komite Politik Alternatif[9] — that are actively advocating an absentee vote on the grounds that neither candidate has solutions. Others — such as the Koalisi Melawan Lupa[10] and Buruh Melawan Lupa[11] — focus their attacks effectively against Prabowo, but without explicitly calling for a vote for Jokowi, on the grounds that he has gross human violators also on his team. These groups represent a small minority among organized forces active in the electoral arena.

However, the question also arises as to whether there are sociological trends that may foster the emergence of alternative outlooks to both what Prabowo and Jokowi stand for, and which the alienated masses may respond to. Over the last few years, the primary new political development that may provide a challenge to the client mentality that is still strong and which could link up with voices that reject what elite politics is currently serving up is the activism of the new labour unions, especially the Metal Workers Federation (FSPMI) and unions working with the FSPMI. It has mobilized hundreds of thousands of mostly factory workers in national actions in 2012 and 2013 — in 2013 in the face of violence from organized anti-union gangs. There are now millions of dues-paying union members who are steadily understanding the usefulness and political potential of mass organizations. In these circles, talk of a new labour party has been increasingly popular. The decision of the FSPMI leadership, taken with no process of mass discussion, to support and campaign strongly for Prabowo, and to enforce discipline to maintain a monolithic line on this despite a clear big vote for the PDIP in the April parliamentary elections in districts where union members reside, has for the moment pressed underground (and into Facebook) discussions of a new party and new political experiments, and even of dissent against the pro-Prabowo line.

However, the emergence of the new unions as a sociological phenomenon and a new political arena will not go away. While there is no guarantee that this will be a fast or smooth process, it is inevitable that the discussion on new parties will re-emerge.

Notes

1. See Max Lane, "Who Will be Indonesian President in 2014", *ISEAS Perspectives*, 18 July 2013.
2. See Max Lane, *Decentralisation and its Discontents: An Essay on Class, Political Agency and National Perspective in Indonesian Politics* (Singapore: Institute of Southeast Asian Studies, 2014) for more discussion on this divide.
3. Ari Dwipoayana, from Gajah mada University, see <http://indonesiasatu. kompas.com/read/2014/06/22/1754152/prabowo-hatta.vs.jokowi-jk.>

mobilisasi.massa.vs.voluntarisme?utm_source=WP&utm_medium=box&utm_ campaign=Kknwp>.

4. <http://m.bisnis.com/pemilu/read/20140606/355/233933/ini-35-jenderal-pendukung-jokowi-jk-5-jenderal-di-duga-bermasalah> lists the 135 retired generals who are supporting Widodo. The Legal Aid Institute lists five as needing to face accusations of gross human rights abuses.

5. <http://politik.news.viva.co.id/news/read/514219-joko-widodo-tidak-setuju-kolom-agama-di-ktp-dihapus>.

6. Edward Aspinall, "Indonesia on the knife's edge", 17 June 2014 <http:// inside.org.au/indonesia-on-the-knifes-edge/> discusses transactional politics and corruption as an explanation for Prabowo's rise in popularity. The article provides a good description of Prabowo's political personality.

7. This was mentioned by Vice-Presidential candidate Yusuf Kalla in the first national debate.

8. See "Memory" in Max Lane, *Unfinished Nation: Indonesia before and after Suharto* (London and New York: Verso, 2008), pp. 91–115.

9. See <http://komitepolitikalternatif.blogspot.sg/>.

10. <http://news.liputan6.com/read/2057539/4-tuntutan-koalisi-melawan-lupa-tragedi-mei-98>.

11. <http://nasional.kompas.com/read/2014/06/13/1359331/Gerakan.Buruh. Melawan.Lupa.Tuntut.KPU.Diskuali-fikasi.Prabowo>.

13

ANALYSING THE ECONOMIC PLATFORMS IN THE INDONESIAN PRESIDENTIAL ELECTION

Maxensius Tri Sambodo and Alexander R. Arifianto

INTRODUCTION

The two sides competing in the Indonesian Presidential election to be held on 9 July — Prabowo Subianto and his Vice Presidential candidate Hatta Rajasa against Joko Widodo (Jokowi) and his running mate Jusuf Kalla — have both submitted their coalition's platforms to the General Elections Commission (KPU).[1]

Whoever becomes president will face the same challenges that outgoing President Susilo Bambang Yudhoyono's (SBY) has been trying to address through his economic policies. These challenges are reflected in the targets

Maxensius Tri Sambodo is Visiting Fellow at ISEAS and researcher at Economic Research Center-Indonesia Institute of Sciences; **Alexander R. Arifianto** is Visiting Fellow at ISEAS. This article was first published on 4 July 2014 as *ISEAS Perspective* 2014/40.

set by the 2014 state budget, which are: (i) to reduce poverty to 9.0–10.5 per cent (currently 11.47 per cent); (ii) to create new jobs (1 per cent economic growth can generate 200,000 new jobs);[2] (iii) to decrease unemployment to 5.7–5.9 per cent (currently 6.25 per cent); and (iv) to decrease income inequality (the Gini coefficient is currently 0.413).

Prabowo's economic strategy is to expand fiscal spending and invest in a range of new development projects with the goal of increasing economic growth to around 7–10 per cent in the first presidential term (2014–19). At the same time, he aims to reduce the Gini ratio to about 0.31. On the other hand, Jokowi proposes to reduce Indonesia's poverty rate to about 5–6 per cent by 2019 by providing free education and skills improvement for the poor.[3]

This article evaluates Prabowo's and Jokowi's proposals in four economic sectors, namely agriculture, energy, industry and labour, which are important for achieving food security, energy security, and enhancing national competitiveness.

GIVING PROMISES

Prabowo proposes a number of new public spending initiatives in his economic platform and plans to increase the public spending-to-GDP-ratio to 19 per cent of GDP by 2019. (The ratio of government spending to GDP during the SBY administration was about 9 per cent.[4]) This means that government spending will increase dramatically under Prabowo's administration, as indicated by his specific proposals. For instance, he plans to increase public investment in basic infrastructure by Rp1,400 trillion (US$98 billion) between 2015 and 2019. His proposal would allocate funds to all public elementary and secondary schools as well as Islamic schools (*pesantrens* or madrasahs) in Indonesia, amounting to Rp150 million (US$12,900) per school. In addition, Prabowo is proposing a new rural development initiative, in which each Indonesian village will receive a direct grant from the national government worth Rp1 billion (US$86,000) to finance village infrastructure projects.

Prabowo's campaign is reliant on increases in public spending and the expansion of state owned enterprises (SOEs), both as direct contractors for the projects and through joint partnerships with the private sector through public-private partnership arrangements. He plans to increase the role of SOEs in development projects, despite how Indonesian state enterprises have had a long history of financial inefficiencies, lower levels of profitability, and are frequently misused as "cash cows" by corrupt government officials.[5]

In turn, the Jokowi platform does not mention macroeconomic targets, but instead outlines detailed and specific targets at the micro level in sectors such as agriculture, energy, transportation, health, education, and services. Jokowi's policies aim to make an impact through using the central government's regulatory powers instead of through direct state expenditures. For instance, he intends to pass seven new laws and revise three laws related to labour and manpower policy. He has also proposed four new legislations to support efforts to fight corruption. Lastly, he plans to amend the Basic Agrarian Law, one of the most complex and controversial Indonesian laws in the books, in order to support his land reform agenda. This reliance on numerous new laws and regulations to support his reforms opens Jokowi to some criticism from those who feel it better for a new government to enforce existing laws and regulations more rigorously than to propose brand new sets of laws and regulations.

AGRICULTURAL SECTOR

There are many overlapping programmes from the two candidates aimed at increasing agricultural input and output. These include expanding the food crop land area, improving farmers' productivity, developing infrastructure, conducting agrarian reform, protecting forest reserves, establishing banks for farmers, fishermen and micro/small enterprises, and developing the marine economy.

The expansion of food crop land area is a complicated task. Prabowo intends to create 2 million hectares of new land for food cultivation, whereas Jokowi intends to create 1 million hectares outside Java and Bali. If one looks to the 1995 Central Kalimantan land clearance project where 1 million hectares of peat land were cleared, land clearance has its own problematic and complex issues (with multi-tiered effects on the environmental, social, cultural, and economic spheres). In that project, there was a lack of infrastructure, seeds, agricultural trainers, and skilled labourers.

Additionally, resultant changes in the environmental ecosystem can also negatively affect such programmes.[6] Furthermore, aggressive agricultural land expansion can threaten forest areas, which would contradict the candidates' goal of conserving Indonesia's remaining forests.

Moreover, both candidates are also committed to carrying out agricultural land reform by redistributing uncultivated lands to small farmers. For example, Jokowi plans to distribute 9 million hectares, and increase land ownership for smallholder farmers from 0.3 hectares to 2 hectares per family. On the other hand, Prabowo wants to put aside 2 million hectares for agricultural production, which can employ up to 12 million people. However, the latest agricultural census indicates that in 2013, 14.25 million households were smallholders (this is defined as land ownership of less than 0.5 hectares) and 68.5 per cent of these live in Java.[7] This implies that since only a limited areas of unused lands are still available in Java, many farmers will need to migrate from Java to other Indonesian islands, which may create communal tensions with the residents of the locales they move to.[8] The census also indicates that agricultural land ownership is being consolidated in the hands of larger landholders.[9] This data implies that future administration in this area will need to take into account the increase in imbalanced land ownership.

ENERGY SECTOR

There are no substantial differences in the presidential candidates' agendas in the energy sector. Both plan to revise the Law on Oil and Gas, promote domestic processing of raw natural resource products, improve Indonesia's energy infrastructure, enhance energy efficiency, promote renewable energy, achieve 100 per cent electrification ratio by 2019, reduce oil subsidy for petrol consumers and renegotiate contracts on mining, oil and gas with multinational mining companies in order to win more concessions for the Indonesian government.

Jokowi plans to promote the use of natural gas for vehicles as a way to replace regular petrol and reduce the costly petrol subsidies. On the other hand, Prabowo proposes to implement price discrimination by imposing a wealth tax on petrol. However, neither of them has publicly advocated increasing petrol prices as part of their strategy to reduce fuel subsidies. Lastly, Prabowo and Jokowi have both pinpointed the importance of renegotiating contracts on mining, oil and gas with foreign companies in order to seek better terms for the Indonesian government. However, it is not known how renegotiations will be conducted and what types of concessions the state wishes to gain from these companies.

INDUSTRIAL SECTOR

Both Jokowi and Prabowo intend to boost Indonesia's currently sluggish manufacturing sector, which has been stagnating since the 1997/98 Asian Financial Crisis,[10] and their ideas for resolving the problem are rather similar. For example, Jokowi promises to achieve "better coordination between national and local government ministries/agencies" while Prabowo proposes to "reduce bureaucratic 'red tape' for obtaining government permits at both national and local levels". To improve industrial policy- making, Jokowi is committed to "building an effective partnership between the public and private sectors" while Prabowo seeks to "improve relations between workers, corporations, and the government". Lastly, both are committed to promoting government support for small and medium-sized enterprises (SMEs) and cooperatives.

The Jokowi campaign is more reliant on developing strategies to promote investment by manufacturing companies. Its platform calls for the provision of tax and fiscal incentives for the manufacturing sector, especially those that "process raw materials or capital-intensive products."[11] On the other hand, the Prabowo faction puts priority on promoting "strategic industries" with the potential to improve Indonesia's fledgling infrastructure. This includes investment in factories that produce transportation vehicles such as automobiles, trains, ships, airplanes, and agricultural-processing vehicles.[12]

However, their proposals do not contain detailed outlines on how exactly they plan to improve the bureaucracy's performance and accountability at both the national and local levels, and on improving relations between the government and the private sector. Better coordination between national and local governments on improving business relations cannot be achieved without removing some of the latter's authority granted by the 2001 Regional Autonomy Law (including the authority to issue investment permits),[13] something that will certainly meet strong resistance from local governments. Lastly, Indonesia's past efforts at promoting investments in "strategic industries" such as automobile have not been successful because these sectors are vulnerable to being captured by powerful bureaucrats and well-connected entrepreneurs who often fail to make these businesses economically viable without constant financial support from the government.[14]

LABOUR SECTOR

The two Presidential candidates' labour platforms share some similar elements but also show some key differences. Jokowi calls for the passage of a series of new laws related to labour policy. These include a law to create a Manpower Supervisory Commission which will enforce existing laws and regulations on labour affairs; a law to establish a National Wage Protection system; and a law to protect the rights of nurses, midwives and household servants. There are also proposals to revise key Indonesian labour laws, such as the Law on Manpower (Law 13/2003), the Law on Industrial Disputes Settlement (Law 2/2004), and the Law on the Placement and Protection of Indonesian Migrant Workers (Law 39/2004). In addition to these laws, Jokowi's platform also calls for the prohibition of outsourcing within state enterprises and for the extension of the National Health Insurance scheme (BJPS) to all Indonesian workers.

However, previous laws and regulations designed to improve workers' salaries and working conditions have often been blamed by the private sector as a source of their high operational costs, which contributes to their reluctance to invest more into the country.[15] While the impact of the proposed legislations is not clear, it is possible that their enactments will increase these costs further.

On the other hand, Prabowo's labour proposal focuses less on the enactment of new laws, and is instead centres on generating 2 million new jobs per year, especially within the agriculture and labor-intensive manufacturing sectors, such as textile, apparel (shoes and garments), and electronic products. However, he does not outline how this initiative is to be financed and whether new supporting legislations will be required.

CONCLUSION

In their economic platforms, both Jokowi and Prabowo emphasize a strong role for the state in the economy. Their approaches differ though. Prabowo proposes an ambitious agenda to promote high economic growth, primarily through public spending increases in the development of infrastructure, education, and agriculture. Jokowi's platform in turn highlights the importance of human resources and food security. For him, retaining and having highly skilled human capital is an important factor in enabling Indonesia to escape the middle income trap and to ease rising income inequality.[16] As mentioned, the many economic initiatives discussed by the two factions are not mutually exclusive and in fact are several ways quite similar.

External observers of this Presidential election should scrutinize both candidates' economic assumptions, spending policies, and legislative proposals in light of the country's economic realities, and the fiscal capabilities of the present Indonesian government. Whoever wins on 9 July 2014 will immediately need to decide on priorities, design more realistic policies and strategies, and promote coordination between relevant ministries and agencies at both the national and local levels. Only then can the country respond more effectively to both domestic and global challenges.

Notes

1. Prabowo's platform seems to be more straightforward while Jokowi's platform has more elaborative statements. Less than a week later, Jokowi's campaign team revised the platform from 41 pages to 12 pages. "Jokowi-JK Padatkan Visi Misi Jadi 12 Halaman" [Jokowi-JK Compressed Platform to 12 pages], <http://nasional.kompas.com/read/2014/05/24/1941484/Jokowi-JK.Padatkan.Visi.Misi.Jadi.12.Halaman> (accessed 25 May 2014).
2. Between February and August 2013, unemployment increased by 220,000 people <http://www.bps.go.id/brs_file/naker_06nov13.pdf> (accessed 26 March 2014).

3. This emphasizes equity as an instrument for sustained economic growth and social as well as political stability <http://www.equityforchildren.org/wp-content/uploads/2013/07/FinalPaper-EquityandSocialJustice-AnIntroduction-1.pdf>; and <http://www.eastwestcenter.org/sites/default/files/private/api101.pdf> (accessed 10 June 2014).

4. Calculating from Pertumbuhan Ekonomi Indonesia 2013 [Indonesia Economic Growth] <http://www.bps.go.id/brs_file/pdb_05feb14.pdf> (accessed 9 June 2014).

5. Only 74 out of 158 SOEs were able to generate a profit in 2006 and about 90 per cent of the profits were contributed by 10 SOEs (Ministry of State-Owned Enterprises, 2006 *Ministerial Report*, Jakarta).

6. "Pembelajaran dari kegagalan penanganan kawasan PLG sejuta hektar menuju pengelolaan lahan gambut berkelanjutan" [Lessoned learn from the failure of 1 million peat area to sustainable peat land management] <http://pustaka.litbang.deptan.go.id/publikasi/ip024091.pdf> (accessed 26 May 2014).

7. "Laporan Hasil Sensus Pertanian" [Report of Agricultural Census in 2013] <http://st2013.bps.go.id/st2013esya/booklet/at0000.pdf> (accessed 27 May 2014).

8. These tensions can be seen from the previous transmigration (*transmigrasi*) programme which was implemented during the New Order regime (1967–98) in order to resettle Javanese farmers to the islands outside of Java. The programme created numerous incidents of communal conflicts and violence, including in Maluku, Papua, Riau, and West Kalimantan. See Jacques Bertrand, *Nationalism and Ethnic Conflict in Indonesia* (New York: Cambridge University Press, 2004) for a study on these conflicts.

9. Central Statistical Agency, op. cit.

10. Haryo Aswicahyo, Hal Hill, and Dionisius Narjoko, *Indonesian Industrialization: A Latecomer Adjusting to Crisis*, World Institute for Development Economics Research (WIDER), Working Paper No. 2011/53 (September 2011). Helsinki: United Nations University <http://labordoc.ilo.org/record/440045> (accessed 28 May 2014).

11. Raw materials producers are primarily mining companies that are mandated under the provisions of Law 4/2009 on Mining and Coal Mining Capital-intensive industries and include producers of non-metallic minerals, steel products, machine goods, electronics, and automobiles. See Aswicahyo, Hill and Narjoko (2011), op. cit., p. 14.

12. Prabowo's proposal resembles the strategy developed by B.J. Habibie, Minister for Research and Technology under former President Suharto (who later succeeded him as President) during the 1980s and 1990s to promote public

investment in "high-technology" industries such as airplanes and commercial ships.

13. Tulus Tambunan. "Inward FDI in Indonesia and Its Policy Context", Columbia FDI Profiles. Vale Columbia Center on Sustainable International Investment, 25 April 2011. New York: Columbia University <http://academiccom-mons.columbia.edu/catalog/ac:135199> (accessed 28 May 2014).

14. For an example of failed efforts by past governments to promote "crucial industries", see Haryo Aswicahyo, M. Chatib Basri, and Hal Hill, "How Not to Industrialize? Indonesia's Automotive Industry", *Bulletin of Indonesian Economic Studies* 36, no. 1 (2000): 209–41.

15. Chris Manning and Kurnya Roesad, "The Manpower Law of 2003 and Its Implementing Regulations: Genesis, Key Articles, and Potential Impact", *Bulletin of Indonesian Economic Studies* 43, no. 1 (2007): 59–86.

16. The middle income trap indicates a stagnancy in income per capita level before crossing to the high-income level.

14

INDONESIAN ISLAMIC PARTIES AFTER THE 2014 ELECTIONS
Divided and Self-Centred

Alexander R. Arifianto

INTRODUCTION

The recently concluded 2014 legislative and presidential elections highlight the continuing importance of Islamic political parties in Indonesian politics. The parties collectively managed to obtain nearly 32 per cent of the vote share in the national legislative election conducted last April. Out of the five Islamic parties contesting, four supported Prabowo Subianto's presidential candidacy, while only one backed Joko Widodo (Jokowi's). What are the roles these parties will play in the new Indonesian government, now that Jokowi is officially the winner of the presidential election and will be inaugurated as Indonesia's new president on 20 October 2014?

The first section of this article reviews the electoral achievements of Islamic political parties in April's legislative election and the ideological and

---

Alexander R. Arifianto is Visiting Fellow at ISEAS.

interest-based differences between these parties. The next section analyses the four largest Islamic parties — the National Awakening Party (PKB), the National Mandate Party (PAN), the Prosperous Justice Party (PKS), and the United Development Party (PPP),[1] discussing whether they will be represented in Jokowi's cabinet, and whether they will likely support or oppose his policy on religious affairs. The final section concludes with some observations on the intermediate prospect of Islamic parties in the new administration.

ELECTORAL RESULTS AND POLITICAL DIVISIONS

Table 1 shows how the five Islamic parties did who competed in the April 2014 legislative election. Collectively, they obtained 31.41 per cent of all the votes cast, surpassing the 25.90 per cent combined vote share they obtained in the 2009 legislative election, which no doubt was a record low for the Islamic parties in post-*reformasi* Indonesian elections.

TABLE 1
Performances of Islamic Parties in the 2014 Indonesian Elections

Party	Ideology	2009 vote share	2014 vote share	Candidate supported
PKB	Moderate, affiliated with NU	4.90%	9.04%	Joko Widodo
PAN	Moderate, affilated with Muhammadiyah	6.00%	7.59%	Prabowo Subianto
PKS	Muslim Brotherhood-influenced Islamists	7.90%	6.79%	Prabowo Subianto
PPP	Conservative Islamists, some NU clerics	5.30%	6.53%	Prabowo Subianto
PBB	Conservative Islamists	1.80%	1.46%	Prabowo Subianto
	Combined vote share of Islamic parties	25.90%	31.41%	

Source: Indonesian Election Commission (KPU) official results, 9 May 2014.

The unexpectedly strong results achieved by the five Islamic parties made some observers wonder about the potentially influential role Islam might have in future Indonesian politics,[2] more specifically, whether it would lead to a stronger push for Islamist agendas — most possibly further restrictions on morality-related matters.[3]

However, this possibility is elusive since the Islamic parties are so divided based on their respective ideologies and political interests. Ideologically, the parties are divided over the interpretation of Islamic teachings and their application in Indonesian society. For instance, PKS is widely believed to support stricter interpretations of Islamic law within Indonesian society and some of its politicians have condoned actions by radical Islamic groups that persecute members of religious minorities.[4] On the other hand, PKB and its sponsoring organization, the Nahdlatul Ulama (NU), advocate an Islamic interpretation that is highly contextualized within Indonesian society, promote tolerance toward Islamic minority sects and non-Muslims, and condemn Islamic radicalism and terrorism.[5]

In addition, despite their support for Prabowo Subianto during the campaigns, many Islamic parties also wish to retain political influence and access to financial patronage in the new Jokowi administration. The official support given by parties such as PAN and PPP to Prabowo are not based on deep ideological similarities, but on the close personal relationship between Prabowo and the party chairmen (Hatta Rajasa for PAN and Suryadharma Ali for PPP). Such support does not necessarily reflect the views of other party politicians and activists, especially those who seek to have a closer relationship with Jokowi in the hope of getting access to political and economic benefits.[6]

As we shall see in the following section, the disagreements between party leaders and activists have resulted in the defections by some activists within PAN to Jokowi's camp and contribute to the infighting that threatens to end Suryadharma Ali's chairmanship within PPP. As a result, while PAN and PPP are currently supporting Prabowo, they might switch their support within the next few months.[7] Since Prabowo has lost his legal challenge against the election results in the Constitutional Court on 21 August 2014, parties seem more likely to focus on their own political interests rather than their coalition's.

INTERNAL DYNAMICS IN THE ISLAMIC PARTIES

Partai Kebangkitan Bangsa (PKB, National Awakening Party)

PKB is affiliated with the Nahdlatul Ulama (NU), Indonesia's largest Islamic organization, which claims to have approximately 50 million sympathizers.[8] It won 9.04 per cent of vote share in last April's legislative election, making it the largest Indonesian Muslim-based party. However, PKB has always been fraught with internal divisions from the time it was founded in 1998. And this year is not an exception. While key leaders such as party chairman Muhaimin Iskandar supported Jokowi, some notable PKB politicians and NU clerics decided to back Prabowo's candidacy instead. They include Mahfud MD, the former Chief Justice of the Indonesian Constitutional Court, and NU chairman Said Agil Siradj. Mahfud was later appointed chairman of Prabowo Subianto's campaign committee (*Tim Sukses* or Success Team). However, he resigned from this position after Jokowi was declared the official winner of the presidential election on 22 July 2014.[9] NU members' supports for Jokowi may have declined further with the publications of "black campaign" pamphlets such as the infamous *Obor Rakyat* ("People's Torch") tabloid.[10]

Despite deep divisions among NU and PKB members during the presidential campaign, the PKB will be benefiting from its alliance with Jokowi, particularly since it was the only Islamic party to support the winning candidate. Emboldened by this prospect, the party has sent a list of ten party cadres that can potentially serve in Jokowi's upcoming cabinet. It also requests to be allocated the position of Minister of Religious Affairs, which historically serves as an important source of financial patronage for the NU.[11] Realistically, however, PKB is only likely to obtain at most three ministerial positions in the new cabinet.[12]

PKB has pledged its support for Jokowi's campaign pledge to promote religious diversity and tolerance in Indonesia. It seeks to achieve it through the promotion of moderate Islamic interpretation in its preaching (*da'wah*) activities and to promote law enforcement actions against those who seek to persecute religious minorities.[13] In addition, Jokowi has appointed Hasyim Muzadi, a former NU chairman, as a special advisor on religious affairs in his transition team.[14] These indicate that the party will use its clout as the largest Muslim-based party in Indonesia to support Jokowi's vision on religious affairs after he assumes office in October 2014.

Partai Amanat Nasional (PAN, National Mandate Party)

PAN is affiliated with the Muhammadiyah, Indonesia's second largest Islamic organization, which claims approximately 30 million sympathizers.[15] It won 7.59 per cent of vote share in last April's legislative election and is the second largest Islamic party in the new Indonesian parliament.

Officially, PAN supported Prabowo Subianto's presidential bid. This decision was largely made by its chairman Hatta Rajasa, who was chosen by Prabowo as his vice presidential running mate. While initially Hatta considered the possibility of aligning PAN with Jokowi, he finally decided to support Prabowo as the latter offered a better deal in terms of possible cabinet ministries and state patronage.[16] However, similar to PKB, not all PAN and Muhammadiyah followers have supported the party's presidential candidate choice. Several notable Muhammadiyah figures, such as its former chairman Syafii Ma'arif and Paramadina University president Anies Baswedan, threw their support behind Jokowi.[17] Thus, while officially PAN was supporting Prabowo's presidential bid, a significant number of its officials differed from their parties' official position, creating tensions within the party.

PAN might eventually switch its support toward Jokowi's coalition. This is because Muhammadiyah prefers to have a representation in any future Indonesian cabinets in order to further promote the organization's development. For instance, the Ministry of Education and Culture, has been led by a minister with Muhammadiyah affiliation since Indonesia's democratic transition in 1999.[18] This tradition will likely continue under the Jokowi administration. It is expected that Anies Baswedan will become the new Minister of Education and Culture as a reward for his support for Jokowi and his role as one of Jokowi's chief spokesperson.[19]

In addition, Jokowi has appointed Syafi'i Ma'arif as one of his special advisor on religious affairs.[20] A prolific scholar whom has published several works on the promotion of moderate Islamic thought, religious minorities, and opposition against Islamic radicalism in Indonesia,[21] he will be influential in shaping Jokowi's religious affairs policy. Since Syafi'i also has an extensive network within the Muhammadiyah as a former chairman of the organization, this indicates that Muhammadiyah can be counted to lend its support for Jokowi's policy as well.

Partai Keadilan Sejahtera (PKS, Prosperous Justice Party)

The PKS is an Islamic party whose ideology is considered similar to revivalist Islamic organizations based in the Middle East, most notably Egypt's Muslim Brotherhood. It won 6.79 per cent of the vote share in the 2014 legislative election, a nearly 1 per cent decrease from its all-time high of 7.90 per cent gained in the 2009 election. The decrease in PKS's vote share was rather minimal compared to the heavily damaged public perception of the party after the "cattle meat imports" corruption scandal involving several key PKS politicians broke, which has resulted in the jailing of its former chairman Luthfi Hasan Ishaaq.[22] However, these allegations do not seem to have affected the fervour of its party cadres, many of whom continue to campaign for its candidates. The efforts of party leaders in framing the scandal as "a political conspiracy to undermine and destroy the party" has also contributed towards keeping the support of its cadres in the 2014 election.[23]

PKS has enthusiastically supported Prabowo Subianto's candidacy from the time it formally endorsed him in May 2014 — possibly because it was promised five cabinet positions.[24] Some PKS activists were allegedly behind the "black campaign" advertisements directed against Jokowi.[25] They purportedly supplied the data used by the Prabowo team to claim victory and challenge the election results in the Constitutional Court.[26]

PKS is widely considered to be the only member of Prabowo's coalition, which would continue to support him and his Gerindra Party in his role as potential opposition against the Jokowi administration. PKS may also oppose Jokowi's efforts to promote religious diversity and tolerance. While some PKS politicians have publicly supported religious pluralism in the past,[27] other party figures have expressed support for provincial and local regulations that persecuted members of Islamic minorities like Ahmadiyah and Shiites,[28] indicating that despite providing "lip service" in support of religious diversity and tolerance, PKS actually might oppose these values.

Partai Persatuan Pembangunan
(PPP, United Development Party)

The PPP was the only legally recognized Islamic party allowed to participate in legislative elections during much of Suharto's New Order regime (1967–98). In the 2014 legislative election, it was able to gain 6.53 per cent of the vote share, a small increase from its 5.3 per cent vote share obtained in the 2009. The party came under scrutiny upon the revelation of a corruption scandal involving party chairman Suryadharma Ali when he was Minister of Religious Affairs. While Suryadharma denied the accusation, he agreed to resign from his cabinet position on 26 May 2014.[29]

A growing number of PPP politicians are distancing themselves from conservatives like Suryadharma. These include Lukman Hakim Saifuddin, the party's deputy chairman who was recently appointed the new Minister of Religious Affairs to succeed Suryadharma on 9 June 2014. As a minister, Lukman Hakim has made positive gestures to religious minorities, for instance by announcing that his ministry is prepared to officially recognize the Baha'i Faith, a religious group widely considered by conservative Muslims to be a deviant sect.[30] This action went in opposition to Suryadharma's actions as Minister of Religious Affairs, whom critics have accused of ignoring and sometimes even condoning, acts of persecution against religious minorities.[31]

If party leadership falls on a moderate politician like Lukman Hakim — who may also stay as minister, PPP's ideological positions can change significantly. It may support Jokowi's efforts to promote moderate Islam and religious tolerance in his new administration. However, this can only happen if the PPP moderates manage to oust Suryadharma in its special national congress that is to be held within the next few months.[32]

CONCLUSION

This article shows that while Islamic parties will continue to play an important role in Indonesian politics, they will remain divided among as well as within themselves. Due to ideological differences, infighting, and diverging politico-economic interests, it is unlikely that Islamic parties can unite to form a viable coalition that can either shift the balance of power or push for legislations that will promote Islamist political interests. The pluralist PKB looks set to significantly increase its influence under the Jokowi administration. Its loyalty is expected to be rewarded with cabinet positions. PKB may also play an important role in Jokowi's religious affairs policy, and be directed to promote religious diversity and tolerance and to crack down on suspected radical Islamic groups. PAN and PPP's future role is contingent upon whether their leaderships decide to switch their allegiances to Jokowi within the next few months. Finally, given its role as a staunch supporter for Prabowo's campaign, PKS is unlikely to switch its support to Jokowi. Instead, it is likely to remain in the opposition against his administration.

Prior to this year's elections, there were numerous concerns among scholars and civil society activists on the future directions of Indonesian Islam. They tended to have a pessimistic outlook due to the rising popularity of conservative movements such as PKS and Hizbut Tahrir Indonesia (HTI),[33] conservative Islamic proselytizing groups in campuses,[34] and more frequent incidents of persecutions against religious minorities.[35] Meanwhile, there have been plenty of criticisms directed against the outgoing Yudhoyono administration for its failure to defend the rights of religious minorities and to take a more assertive action against radical Islamic groups who are persecuting them.[36]

However, the result of the presidential election seems to indicate that moderate Islam in Indonesia is more resilient than originally thought. A majority of Indonesians voted for Jokowi, who seems committed to promoting moderate expressions of Islam, and protecting religious minorities, and is less likely to tolerate the actions of radical Islamic groups. Put simply, the elections seem to have decreased the popularity of conservative Islamic parties such as PKS and bolstered support towards more moderate parties such as PKB. With these developments, there is greater likelihood that civil and moderate Islam will have a stronger role to play during Jokowi's tenure.

Notes

1. This analysis excludes PBB, the fifth Islamic Party, because it did not reach the legally mandated electoral threshold of 3.5 per cent of votes casted in

the legislative election and it failed to win any seats in the new Indonesian Parliament (DPR).

2. For instance, see Agence-France Presse, "Islamic Parties Bounce Back in Muslim-Majority Indonesia's Parliamentary Elections", *South China Morning Post*, 11 April 2014 <http://www.scmp.com/news/asia/article/1475955/islamic-parties-bounce-back-muslim-majority-indonesias-parliamentary> (accessed 14 April 2014).

3. While there is no prospect for the adoption of a national *shari'a* law in Indonesia in the immediate future, one province (Aceh Special Autonomous Province) and fifty-two districts and municipalities have enacted local *shari'a* regulations within their territories. In addition, numerous Indonesian districts and municipalities have adopted "morality" regulations such as prohibitions on the sale of alcoholic beverages and prostitution, and the *hijab* (veiling) requirements for Muslim women, that were strongly influenced by *shari'a* law. For further details, see Robin Bush, "Regional Shari'a Regulations in Indonesia: Anomaly of Symptoms?", in *Expressing Islam: Religious Life and Politics in Indonesia*, edited by Greg Fealy and Sally White (Singapore: Institute of Southeast Asian Studies, 2008), pp. 174–91.

4. PKS leaders such as its former chairman Hidayat Nur Wahid said that while the party rejects the broad implementation of *shari'a* law in Indonesia, it supports the enactment of certain "moral enhancement" clauses of the *shari'a* (Bush, op cit., p. 175). Politicians affiliated with PKS have either condoned or actively participated in acts of persecutions against religious minorities such as Christians, Shiites, and Ahmaddiyah sect. For instance, see Camelia Pasandaran, "Hard-Liners to Host Anti Shia Declaration, West Java Governor to Attend", *Jakarta Globe*, 16 April 2014 <http://www.thejakartaglobe.com/news/hard-liners-host-anti-shiite-declaration-w-java-governor-attend/> (accessed 22 August 2014).

5. For instance, NU Chairman Said Agil Siradj said that his organization opposeses any acts of radicalism and terrorism in the name of Islam. Instead, he argies that "NU members must show tolerance toward people from other faith traditions, as the Qur'an asks all Muslims to do so". Aseanty Pahlevi, "Ini Kata Said Agil Soal Al Qur'an dan Toleransi" [This is Said Agil's Statement about Al Qur'an and Tolerance], Tempo.co, 4 July 2012 <http://www.tempo.co/read/news/2012/07/04/173414683/Ini-Kata-Said-Agil-Soal-Al-Quran-dan-Toleransi> (accessed 22 August 2014).

6. For more on this, see Greg Fealy, "Uneasy Alliance: Prabowo and the Islamic Parties", *New Mandala*, College of Asia and the Pacific, Australian National University, 9 July 2014 <http://asiapacific.anu.edu.au/newmandala/

2014/07/09/uneasy-alliance-prabowo-and-the-islamic-parties/> (accessed 18 August 2014).
7. This can be seen clearly in the case of PPP. See Ahmad Toriq, "Prabowo Kalah, PPP Terpecah Belah" [Prabowo Loses, PPP is Completely Divided], detikNews. com, 18 August 2014 <http://news.detik.com/pemilu2014/read/2014/08/18/100138/2664821/1562/prabowo-kalah-ppp-terpecah-belah?991104topnews> (accessed 20 August 2014).
8. Sumanto al Qurtuby, "Nahdlatul Ulama: Good Governance and Religious Tolerance in Indonesia", Kroc Institute of International Peace Studies, University of Notre Dame, 15 January 2013 <http://blogs.nd.edu/contendingmodernities/2013/01/15/nahdlatul-ulama-good-governance-and-religious-tolerance-in-indonesia/> (accessed 4 March 2014).
9. Although Mahfud has indicated that he felt "used" by Muhaimin Iskandar for PKB's campaign, according to a Mahfud confidant, the main reason why he decided to back Prabowo instead of Jokowi was because the former promised to name him to a senior ministerial position in his cabinet, most likely as the Coordinating Minister for Political and Security Affairs (*Menko Polkam*) (Confidential interview with Mahfud MD's senior aide, Jakarta, 19 June 2014). However, some also speculate that Mahfud decided to support Prabowo because he was disappointed for not being selected as Jokowi's Vice Presidential running mate, instead of the eventual nominee, former Vice President Jusuf Kalla. Ferdinand Waskita, "Jadi Timses Prabowo, PKB Sebut Mahfud MD Sedang Kecewa" [Joining Prabowo's Success Team, PKB Official States that Mahfud MD is Feeling Disappointed], Tribunnews.com, 20 May 2014 <http://www.tribunnews.com/pemilu-2014/2014/05/20/jadi-timses-prabowo-hatta-pkb-sebut-mahfud-md-sedang-kecewa> (accessed 25 August 2014).
10. The tabloid, allegedly funded by the Prabowo campaign was distributed to NU-sponsored *pesantren* (Islamic boarding schools) and carried false allegations against Jokowi, for instance, alleging he was actually an ethnic Chinese Christian, instead of a Javanese Muslim. NU Online, "Obor Rakyat Serbu Pesantren-Pesantren Tanpa Alamat Pengirim" [Obor Rakyat 'Attacks' Islamic Boarding Schools without a Return Address], 28 June 2014 <http://www.nu.or.id/a,public-m,dinamic-s,detail-ids,44-id,52927-lang,id-c,nasional-t,Obor+Rakyat+Serbu+Pesantren+pesantren+Tanpa+Alamat+Pengirim-.phpx> (accessed 18 August 2014).
11. The current Religious Affairs Minister is Lukman Hakim Saifuddin from the PPP. Mulya Nubilikis, "PKB Singgung Jatah Menteri Agama, Ini Kata Jokowi" [PKB Requests the Religious Affairs Ministry; This is Jokowi's Response],

detikNews.com, 5 August 2014 <http://news.detik.com/pemilu2014/read/2014/08/05/125751/2653605/1562/pkb-singgung-jatah-menteri-agama-ini-kata-jokowi> (accessed 18 August 2014).

12. The speculation is that three cabinet positions may be given to its chairman Muhaimin Iskandar, its vice-chairman, Indonesian Chinese businessman Rusdi Kirana and Imam Nahrawi, the party's general secretary. Solopos.com, "Elite Parpol Ingin Masuk Kabinet? Ini Tantangan Jokowi" [Party Elites want to enter the Cabinet? This is Jokowi's Challenge], 9 August 2014 <http://www.solopos.com/2014/08/09/jokowi-presiden-elite-parpol-ingin-masuk-kabinet-ini-tantangan-jokowi-525100> (accessed 18 August 2014).

13. Firardy Rozy, "PKB Pastikan Jokowi Pertahankan Pluralisme" [PKB Will Ensure Jokowi to Defend Religious Pluralism]. *Rakyat Merdeka Online*, 12 June 2014 <http://politik.rmol.co/read/2014/06/12/159222/PKB-Pastikan-Jokowi-JK-Pertahankan-Pluralisme-> (accessed 22 June 2014).

14. Kompas.com, "Jokowi Ajak Hasyim Muzadi dan Syafii Ma'arif sebagai Penasihat Tim Transition" [Jokowi Asks Hasyim Muzadi and Syafii Ma'arif to be Advisers in His Transition Team], 11 August 2014 <http://nasional.kompas.com/read/2014/08/11/22491361/Jokowi.Ajak.Hasyim.Muzadi.dan.Syafii.Maarif.sebagai.Penasihat.Tim.Transisi> (accessed 23 August 2014).

15. Saiful Mujani and R. William Liddle, "Muslim Indonesia's Secular Democracy", *Asian Survey* 49, no. 4 (July/August 2009): 580.

16. Greg Fealy, "Uneasy Alliance: Prabowo and the Islamic Parties", *New Mandala*, College of Asia and the Pacific, Australian National University, 9 July 2014 <http://asiapacific.anu.edu.au/newmandala/2014/07/09/uneasy-alliance-prabowo-and-the-islamic-parties/> (accessed 18 August 2014).

17. Solopos.com, "Syafii Ma'arif Dukung Jokowi Jadi Presiden, Bagaimana Muhammadiyah?" [Syafii Ma'arif Endorses Jokowi as President, How about Muhammadiyah?], 3 May 2014 <http://www.solopos.com/2014/05/03/jokowi-capres-syafii-maarif-dukung-jokowi-jadi-presiden-bagaimana-muhammadiyah-505808> (accessed 25 August 2014).

18. The four Ministers for Education and Culture who assumed office since 1999 were all affiliated with Muhammadiyah. They were: Yahya Muhaimin (1999–2001), Abdul Malik Fajar (2001–04), Bambang Sudibyo (2004–09), and Mohammad Nuh (2009–14). Malik Fajar is currently a member of Muhammadiyah's leadership board (*PP Muhammadiyah*).

19. Anies' name is listed as a prospective Minister for Education and Culture in the numerous unofficial lists of Jokowi's cabinet ministers circulated among Indonesian news media since Jokowi became a presidential candidate. For instance, see Rahmat Fiansyah, "PDI-P Bantah Susunan Kabinet Trisakti untuk

Jokowi-JK" [PDI-P Denies Forming the 'Trisakti' Cabinet for Jokowi-JK], Kompas. com, 12 May 2014 <http://nasional.kompas.com/read/2014/05/12/1707219/ PDI-P.Bantah.Susunan.Kabinet.Trisakti.untuk.Jokowi-JK> (accessed 19 August 2014).

20. Kompas.com, "Jokowi Ajak Hasyim Muzadi dan Syafii Ma'arif sebagai Penasihat Tim Transition" [Jokowi Asks Hasyim Muzadi and Syafii Ma'arif to be Advisers in His Transition Team], 11 August 2014 <http://nasional. kompas.com/read/2014/08/11/22491361/Jokowi.Ajak.Hasyim.Muzadi.dan. Syafii.Maarif.sebagai.Penasihat.Tim.Transisi> (accessed 23 August 2014).

21. For instance, see Ahmad Syafii Ma'arif. *Islam dalam Bingkai Keindonesiaan dan Kemanusiaan* [Islam under the Frameworks of Indonesianness and Humanity] (Bandung, Indonesia: PT Mizan Publika, 2009).

22. Dimas Siregar, "Suara Jeblok, Demokrat dan PKS Dihukum Pemilih" [Vote Share Declining, Democratic Party and PKS are Punished by Voters], Tempo.co, 10 April 2014 <http://pemilu.tempo.co/read/news/2014/04/10/269569549/ Suara-Jebloki-Demokrat-dan-PKS-Dihukum-Pemilih> (accessed 19 August 2014).

23. Sabrina Acil, "Anis Matta Tuding Ada Konspirasi Besar untuk Serang PKS" [Anis Matta Alleges a 'Great Conspiracy' to Attack PKS], Kompas.com, 1 February 2013 <http://nasional.kompas.com/read/2013/02/01/16172470/Anis.Matta. Tuding.Ada.Konspirasi.Besar.untuk.Serang.PKS> (accessed 12 April 2014).

24. Danu Damarjati and Idham Khalid, "Beredar Susunan Kabinet Prabowo-Hatta, Gerindra: Itu Tidak Benar" [Prabowo-Hatta Cabinet List is Circulated, Gerindra: It is not True], detikNews.com, 13 May 2014, <http://news.detik. com/pemilu2014/read/2014/05/13/134224/2581258/1562/beredar-susunan-kabinet-prabowo-hatta-gerindra-itu-nggak-benar?9911012> (accessed 19 August 2014).

25. For instance, the infamous Jokowi's mock obituary which indicated that he was a Christian of Chinese descent instead of a Javanese Muslim, was originally posted by the party's social media affiliate called *PKS Piyungan*. Jafar Sodiq Assegaf, "Tertuduh Penyebar 'RIP Jokowi' Akhirnya Buka Suara, Salahkan PKS Piyungan" [Alleged Leaker of "RIP Jokowi" Ad Finally Speaks Out, Blames *PKS Piyungan* Site], Solopos.com, 13 May 2014 <http://www.solopos. com/2014/05/13/kampanye-hitam-capres-tertuduh-penyebar-rip-jokowi-akhirnya-buka-suara-salahkan-pks-piyungan-507457> (accessed 19 August 2014).

26. Metrotvnews.com, "Hasto: Mungkinkah PKS Rekayasa Data supaya Prabowo Senang?" [Hasto: Is It Possible that PKS Falsifies Its Data to Make Prabowo Happy?], 11 July 2014 <http://pemilu.metrotvnews.com/

read/2014/07/11/264368/hasto-mungkinkah-pks-rekayasa-data-supaya-prabowo-senang> (accessed 19 August 2014).

27. Fabian Januarius Kuwado, "Hidayat Nur Wahid soal Pluralisme di Jakarta" [Hidayat Nur Wahid on Religious Pluralism in Jakarta], Kompas.com, 20 March 2012 <http://megapolitan.kompas.com/read/2012/03/20/07074670/Hidayat. Nurwahid.soal.Pluralisme.di.Jakarta)> (accessed 22 August 2014).

28. For instance, West Java Governor Ahmad Heryawan, a PKS politician, attended an event sponsored by a local alliance of radical Islamic groups called the Anti Shia Alliance, which declared Shiism as a heretical Islamic sect that should be prohibited within the province. Camelia Pasandaran, "Hard-Liners to Host Anti Shia Declaration, West Java Governor to Attend", *Jakarta Globe*, 16 April 2014 <http://www.thejakartaglobe.com/news/hard-liners-host-anti-shiite-declaration-w-java-governor-attend/> (accessed 22 August 2014).

29. Prihandoko, "Suryadharma Akhirnya Mundur dari Kabinet SBY") [Suryadharma Finally Resigns from SBY's Cabinet], Tempo.co, 26 May 2014 <http://www.tempo.co/read/news/2014/05/26/063580455/Suryadharma-Akhirnya-Mundur-dari-Kabinet-SBY> (accessed 19 August 2014).

30. Camelia Pasandaran, "New Religious Affairs Minister Supports State Recognition of Baha'i Religion", *Jakarta Globe*, 25 July 2014 <http://www.thejakartaglobe.com/news/new-religious-affairs-minister-supports-state-recognition-bahai-religion/> (accessed 22 August 2014).

31. Josua Gantan, "Religious Affairs Minister Suryadharma Doubts Claims of Intolerance in Indonesia", *Jakarta Globe*, 9 June 2014 <http://www.thejakartaglobe.com/news/religious-affairs-minister-suryadharma-doubts-claims-of-intolerance-in-indonesia/> (accessed 22 August 2014).

32. Ahmad Toriq, "Prabowo Kalah, PPP Terpecah Belah" [Prabowo Loses, PPP is Completely Divided], detikNews.com, 18 August 2014 <http://news.detik.com/pemilu2014/read/2014/08/18/100138/2664821/1562/prabowo-kalah-ppp-terpecah-belah?991104topnews> (accessed 20 August 2014).

33. Martin van Bruinessen, ed., *Contemporary Developments in Indonesian Islam: Explaining the "Conservative Turn"* (Singapore: Institute of Southeast Asian Studies, 2013).

34. Leonard C. Sebastian, Jonathan Chen, and Emirza Adi Syaliendra, *Pemuda Rising: Why Indonesia Should Pay Attention to Its Youth*. RSIS Monograph No. 29 (Singapore: S. Rajaratnam School of International Studies, 2014). Available at <https://www.rsis.edu.sg/rsis-publication/idss/pemuda-rising-why-indonesia-should-pay-attention-to-its-youth/#.U_w6_6NafTo> (accessed 26 August 2014).

35. Human Rights Watch, *In Religions' Name: Abuses against Religious Minorities*

in Indonesia, 28 February 2013 <http://www.hrw.org/reports/2013/02/28/religion-s-name-0> (accessed 26 August 2014).

36. Human Rights Watch, op. cit. See also Phelim Kine, "President Yudhoyono's Blind Spot: Religious Violence in Indonesia", *Jakarta Globe*, 25 August 2014 <http://www.thejakartaglobe.com/opinion/president-yudhoyonos-blind-side-religious-violence-indonesia/> (accessed 26 August 2014).

15

SAFEGUARDING INDONESIA'S PLURALISM
An Essential Task for Joko Widodo

Gwenael Njoto-Feillard

INTRODUCTION

As the largest Muslim-majority country and the fourth most populous nation in the world, Indonesia has often been cited as an example of Islam, democracy and economic development coexisting.[1] However, while the country has long been hailed for its tolerant form of Islam, the pluralistic model of Indonesian society has been threatened by the growth of religious intolerance in recent years.[2] While members from the Jemaah Islamiyah have been hunted down, shot by the police or thrown into prison, the Indonesian authorities under President Yudhoyono have been much less adamant in protecting the rights of religious minorities

Gwenael Njoto-Feillard is Visiting Fellow at ISEAS.

and bringing to justice the various radical groups that have perpetrated violent acts against them.[3]

On 9 July 2014 Indonesians voted in their fifth president since the fall of the Suharto regime in 1998. This article investigates the prospects of the new Jokowi-Kalla administration in light of problems of growing sectarianism in Indonesia. Indeed, with the election of Joko Widodo, Indonesia may have avoided a possible return to authoritarian rule, but also a further increase of tensions around religious issues. The president-elect's rival, Prabowo Subianto is known to have had links with radical elements of Indonesian Islam since the mid-1990s.[4] It is therefore not surprising that, during the campaign, Islamist parties and radical groups threw their weight behind the Prabowo-Hatta ticket, hoping that their demand for a greater Islamization of Indonesian society would be accepted. As an example, the Islamic Defenders Front (FPI, Front Pembela Islam), while first hesitant to support Prabowo, later called to vote for him, hoping that he would favour the growth of local sharia by-laws (*perda syari'ah*). With the Constitutional Court's decision to confirm Jokowi's victory on 21 August, it will never be known whether an elected Prabowo would have turned his back on his Islamist and neo-fundamentalist supporters or, on the contrary, if he would have bought social peace by giving in to their demands.

However, what is certain now is that Joko Widodo and Jusuf Kalla face an important and difficult task in preserving one of the county's main assets — its pluralist and tolerant model — while carefully managing the possible tensions created by the rapidly changing religious landscape of Indonesian society.

THE MANY EXPECTATIONS ON THE JOKOWI PRESIDENCY

While he can claim economic development as one of his achievements, President Yudhoyono has clearly failed in protecting the rights of religious minorities and curtailing the growth of ultra-conservative elements within Indonesian Islam. Many local NGOs expressed surprise when, in May 2013, President Yudhoyono received an award from a U.S.-based interfaith organization for his achievements in promoting tolerance and freedom of worship in Indonesia.[5] Indeed, for years, hate speech and repeated attacks against Christians and Muslim minority sects (Ahmadiyyah, Shias and more recently some Sufis) by groups such as the Front Pembela Islam (FPI, Islamic Defenders Front) and the Forum Umat Islam (FUI, Islamic People's Forum) have gone largely unanswered. While Yudhoyono can be considered a moderate Muslim, his persistent inaction has given the radicals legitimacy by default.

Coming from a Javanese *abangan* (nominal Muslim) background, the president might have felt that he did not have enough religious clout to come down hard on the radicals. More importantly, his coalition of parties included conservative elements of Indonesian Islam[6] who would have reacted rather negatively to clampdown. In this sense, violent radical elements and institutionalised Islamism found common ideological ground, even if this is not always acknowledged openly.

Another source of indirect legitimacy for the radicals' attacks on minorities came from the Indonesian Council of Ulamas (MUI, Majelis Ulama Indonesia). Created in 1971 by the Suharto government to legitimize its rule in religious affairs, the MUI has taken centre-stage in Post-New Order Indonesia in trying to establish itself as the authoritative institution of religious orthodoxy.[7] In this effort, it has adopted a conservative position on a number of issues pertaining to religious freedom. In a 2005 legal advices (*fatwa*), MUI prohibited pluralism, secularism and liberalism.[8] The same year it declared that the Ahmadiyya community had deviated from Quranic teachings and asked the government to outlaw the group. This fatwa was later used by radicals to legitimise violence.[9]

Even more disturbing is the fact that the source of the problem during the last tenure of Yudhoyono has been the Ministry for Religious Affairs itself. Then-Minister Suryadharma Ali, from the United Development Party (PPP, Partai Persatuan Pembangunan), was often accused by NGOs of keeping a blind eye on various attacks on religious minorities, thus emboldening the radical groups even more.[10] Now under investigation by the Corruption Eradication Commission (KPK) for his involvement in the misuse of Haj funds, Suryadharma has since June 2014 been replaced by Lukman Hakim Saifuddin. After being sworn in, Lukman has shown a clear willingness to promote dialogue among the country's religious traditions. He even introduced the possibility of discussing state recognition of the Baha'i faith to be included among the country's six official religions. This change of leadership at the Ministry of Religious Affairs can thus be considered a welcome development and a possible sign of changing times.

Indeed, while foreign and local observers have noted that the 2014 elections have been a great achievement for Indonesian democracy, Jokowi's win must be considered a victory for moderate Islam as well. These elections were marked by a never before seen polarisation, with a ruthless black campaign being carried out against Jokowi. He was accused of being a Chinese and a Christian, and working for the interests of America, Israel and the Vatican — in short, an "infidel" (*kafir*) and an enemy of Islam. These personal attacks may have convinced Jokowi even more of the necessity of defending Indonesia's pluralistic model of religious harmony during his future tenure. In one speech, he reaffirmed the ideal religion that he envisioned for himself and for Indonesia:

> I am Jokowi, part of an Islam that is a "blessing for all mankind" (*rahmatan lill alamin*). An Islam that lives through heritage of and works through the Indonesian Republic, and holds firmly to the 1945 Constitution. "Unity in diversity" (the national motto of Indonesia) is a gift from God...
>
> I am not part of that Islam that tramples other religions. I am not part of that Islam that is arrogant and draws the sword to hand and mouth.... I am not part of that group within Islam that makes, with such ease, his own brother an heretic.[11]

This was the first time in recent Indonesia history that such an important political figure, from a secular-nationalist party (PDI-P), had dare to speak so boldly in defence of moderate Islam, while directly attacking the radicals' ideology and actions.

It remains to be seen how Jokowi's words will be put into action, and in this effort, his party, the PDI-P, will probably be an important source of support. While under the influence of Megawati's late husband Taufiq Kiemas (who passed away in June 2013), the PDI-P tried to Islamize its image to further appeal to Muslim voters through the creation of a department in charge of Islamic affairs, the "Indonesian Muslim House" (Baitul Muslimin Indonesia). Now in full control, Megawati is known for her personal dislike of strongly ideologically-oriented Islamist parties such as the Prosperous Justice Party (PKS, Partai Keadilan Sejahtera).

In defending his view of a plural and tolerant society, a key issue for Jokowi will be the nominations to ministerial posts. Held during Yudhoyono's second term by a PKS figure, Tifatul Sembiring, the Ministry of Information has been accused of pursuing a restrictive moralising agenda while letting radical content flow freely on the internet (known to be an important arena for the recruitment for extremists). Evidently, another key post is the Ministry of Religious affairs. Because the PKB, affiliated to the traditionalist organization NU, had supported the Jokowi-Kalla ticket from the start, many observers suggest the likelihood of a figure proposed by PKB (at the very least coming from traditionalist Islam) being nominated to the post, which would bring a stronger push for moderate Islam.[12] The new president will indeed have to count on Islamic civil society — of which NU is part — to pursue his agenda on tolerance and pluralism.

CIVIL ISLAM AND THE CHALLENGE OF RADICALISM

Since the early twentieth century, Indonesia's two largest Muslim organizations, the traditionalist Nahdlatul Ulama and the modernist Muhammadiyah, have been key players in the social and religious transformation of the country. With millions of members, thousands of branches, hospitals, universities, schools and orphanages, they have been strongly influencing Indonesian Islam. At the end of the 1990s, with the fall of Suharto and the opening up of the country through democratic reforms, this quasi-monopoly has been seriously challenged. The "market" of spirituality is now much more open and the growing demand for piety within society has been answered by a more diverse scope on "offer" in terms of religious participation and affiliation with newcomer groups.[13]

Moreover, the two organizations have been confronted more recently from within their own ranks, by what Martin van Bruinessen has called a "conservative turn" in Indonesian Islam.[14] While their leadership has often defended a moderate position, grassroots members seem to show more conservative orientations. This has probably facilitated the strategy of new Islamist and neo-fundamentalist organisations such as the PKS and the transnational organisation Hizbut Tahrir to penetrate NU and Muhammadiyah institutions and enlist their members. In reaction, NU and Muhammadiyah leaders have more recently adopted a stricter policy of membership and activities. More importantly, it seems that with the chaos and violence marking many parts of the Muslim world, especially since 2011, both organisations have realised the importance of defining and asserting an Islam that is rooted in the local socio-cultural context, one that rejects violence and values tolerance.[15]

As noted by Robert Hefner, these two major components of Indonesian Islam, NU and Muhammadiyah, are probably unique in the Muslim world in that, very early on, they have reflected and, more importantly, acted systematically for the advancement of the "public interest" (*maslahah*) on a nationwide scale through their millions of sympathizers and thousands of branches and institutions.[16] By occupying the socio-religious space, they have also been relatively successful in acting as a buffer against the tactics of charitable works, a classic tool of Islamism and neo-fundamentalism in the Middle East.[17] Through a number of affiliated institutes, they have been active in reflecting, publishing and mediating their views on peace and tolerance among religions. As an example, the Centre for Dialogue and Cooperation among Civilizations, initiated by Muhammadiyah chairman Din Syamsuddin, organized recently a talk on Islam-Buddhism relations in Southeast Asia to try and mitigate the tensions created by the violence against Rohyingas in Myanmar.[18] The Muhammadiyah-affiliated Centre has also been active in discreetly providing humanitarian assistance to the displaced Shia community of Sampang (Madura, East Java) which was victim of violence throughout 2012.

There is now a general understanding, both in these socio-religious organizations and in the government, that the battle for the hearts of Muslims is held first in the field of ideas and ideology. It was long considered that radicalism was either a construction of the West to discredit Islam or an epiphenomenon that was best ignored and left to die down on its own. This evidently did not happen. First focused on deradicalization programmes for militants in prison, the government seems now more open to a preventive approach. In Bekasi (West Java), it has opened the first school to promote pluralism and tolerance among communities, integrating a programme based on the Pancasila, the philosophical foundation of the Indonesian state. It is interesting to note that while the Pancasila has often been criticized in the Post-Suharto years as ideological control of Islamic organisations, it has made a significant comeback in recent years and is being defended by both the NU and Muhammadiyah.[19]

This idea of an Indonesian cultural specificity centred around the values of the Pancasila has been used to counter the growing threat in Indonesia of the "Islamic State of Iraq and the Levant" (now shortened to "Islamic State"), an organization whose aim is to establish a world caliphate. For many months, IS activists have been raising money and recruiting new members, and swearing allegiance (bai'at) to the caliphate's leader, Abu Bakr al-Baghdadi. As terrorism expert Sidney Jones has suggested, it is doubtful that IS will make any significant gain in Indonesia.[20] Its ultra-violence is a clear deterrent, but it should be noted that its transnationalism has rebuked many as well. Interestingly, this has forced other organizations known to promote the model of the caliphate to clarify their position on the matter, as in the case with the Hizbut Tahrir Indonesia (HTI).[21] While the HTI has been quite intense in its criticism of democracy, it has also insisted that it rejects any form of violence.[22]

Overall, almost all Islamic parties and organizations in Indonesia have condemned the Islamic State (IS).[23] Even the conservative-leaning Council of Indonesian Ulamas (MUI) has issued a strong statement against the movement. Reactions against IS have not been limited to the political or the religious elites, and have extended to some local communities as well. In Pekayon (Bekasi, West Java), a mosque was recently taken back from IS sympathizers by the local Muslim population. It seems that the main challenge to the growth of this brand of radical Islam in Indonesia is also its exclusivist and nihilistic orientation. The fact that IS intends to destroy all symbols of local Islamic culture is probably a strong deterrent for Indonesian Muslims.

While its model of tolerance has been challenged in recent years, Indonesian Islam has shown relatively high resilience to the growth of radicalism — a capacity that needs to be further reinforced by the state in cooperation with different elements of civil society. The government needs urgently to solve the issue of displaced communities who live in dire conditions after being victims of violence, such as the 100 or more Ahmadiyya followers in Mataram (Lombok).[24] Extremist ideologies from any religious tradition should be curtailed and strict enforcement of the law put into practice. Activists have suggested that article 156 of the Criminal

Code pertaining to hate speech could be amended to more clearly include the religious factor.[25] Because radical views are reinforced by ignorance and/or misunderstanding, education is evidently key. A better knowledge of different religions could be taught in secular schools, but probably also in religious institutions, such as the thousands of Islamic boarding schools (*pesantren*) spread throughout the country.

With these objectives in mind, the Jokowi administration can work with and support institutionally and financially the country's two largest Muslim organizations, the Nahdlatul Ulama and the Muhammadiyah. Young activists from these two organizations are often fluent in Arabic and have detailed knowledge of Islamic texts, which allows them to articulate an effective argumentation against sectarianism. Having benefited from overseas scholarships, some come back to Indonesia with a global experience that makes them key to furthering this essential brand of Islam that is pluralistic and moderate.

CONCLUSION

A new agenda for safeguarding a pluralist and tolerant society is needed in Indonesia. This is all the more important since, with the political upheavals and mounting communitarian conflicts in many parts of the Muslim world, the country now draws more and more attention from the international community. Indonesia needs to institutionalize its model as an asset that can be used to promote its growing geostrategic importance in the Muslim world, but also on the global stage. While Malaysia has used Islamic economics to recentre its position in the Muslim world, Indonesia can do so through its democratic and pluralistic society.

Notes

1. "Obama hails Indonesia as an example for the world", bbc.co.uk, 10 November 2010 <http://www.bbc.co.uk/news/world-asia-pacific-11723650>; "Clinton praises Indonesian democracy", Nytimes.com, 18 February 2009 <http://www.nytimes.com/2009/02/19/washington/19diplo.html?_r=0>.
2. See Human Rights Watch's 2013 report "In religion's name: Abuses against religious minorities in Indonesia" <http://www.hrw.org/news/2013/02/28/indonesia-religious-minorities-targets-rising-violence>.

3. <http://www.thejakartaglobe.com/opinion/president-yudhoyonos-blind-side-religious-violence-indonesia/>.
4. Prabowo had approached the DDII and the KISDI in support of President Suharto fledging grip on power.
5. "SBY's pluralist legacy in tatters, survey confirms", JakartaGlobe.com, 23 April 2014 <http://www.thejakartaglobe.com/news/sbys-pluralist-legacy-tatters-survey-confirms>.
6. The PKS (Prosperous Justice Party) and the PPP (United Development Party).
7. Moch Nur Ichwan, "Towards a Puritanical Moderate Islam: The Majelis Ulama Indonesia and the Politics of Religious Orthodoxy", in *Contemporary Developments in Indonesian Islam: Explaining the Conservative Turn*, edited by Martin van Bruinessen (Singapore: Institute of Southeast Asian Studies, 2013).
8. Piers Gillespie, "Current Issues in Indonesian Islam: Analysing the 2005 Council of Indonesian Ulama Fatwa No. 7 Opposing Pluralism, Liberalism and Secularism", *Journal of Islamic Studies* 18, no. 2 (1 May 2007): 202–40.
9. "MUI fatwa feeds flames of cleric's hate speech", TheJakartaPost.com, 17 January 2011 <http://www.thejakartapost.com/news/2011/01/17/mui-fatwa-feeds-flames-clerics%E2%80%99-hate-speech.html>.
10. "The paradox of Indonesia's democracy and religious freedom", Freedomhouse. org, 21 June 2012 <http://www.freedomhouse.org/blog/paradox-indonesia%E2%80%99s-democracy-and-religious-freedom#.U_whs7x_tZM>.
11. "Saya Jokowi, Bagian dari Islam yang Rahmatan Lil Alamin" [I am Jokowi, part of an Islam that is a blessing for all mankind], Kompas.com, 24 May 2004 <http://nasional.kompas.com/read/2014/05/24/1429414/.Saya.Jokowi.Bagian.dari.Islam.yang.Rahmatan.Lil.Alamin>.
12. The PDI-P has recently declared that it was favourable to keeping Lukman Hakim Saifuddin at the head of the Ministry during Jokowi's tenure <http://nasional.kompas.com/read/2014/08/25/18233841/PDI-P.Ingin.Lukman.Hakim.Jadi.Menteri.Agama.dalam.Pemerintahan.Jokowi-JK>.
13. For example, the Emotional Spiritual Quotient (ESQ) movement, created by Ari Ginanjar, is considered to be a mix between Sufism and managerial psychology; or, on the other side of the spectrum, the Jemaah Tabligh, an apolitical and puritan movement focused on itinerant proselytizing (created in 1926 in India, as an offshoot of the Deobandi movement).
14. Martin van Bruinessen, *Contemporary Developments in Indonesian Islam: Explaining the "Conservative Turn"* (Singapore: Institute of Southeast Asian Studies, 2013).

15. For the NU, this evolution is even more significant. The traditionalist organization is being challenged by Wahhabi-inspired preachers who used to operate mainly in Central Java, but who are now actively moving to East Java, the stronghold of NU. Interviews with various members of the NU leadership in Surabaya, June 2014.

16. *Studia Islamika* journal 20-years anniversary, UIN Campus, Jakarta, 13–15 August 2014.

17. Vedi R Hadiz, "No Turkish Delight: The Impasse of Islamic Party Politics in Indonesia", *Indonesia*, no. 92 (2011): 1–18.

18. The talk featured respected scholar, Professor Imtiyaz Yusuf from Mahidol University, and representatives of the Indonesian Buddhist community (23 August 2014, Jakarta) <http://www.cdccfoundation.org/>.

19. François Raillon, "The Return of Pancasila: Secular vs. Islamic Norms, Another Look at the Struggle for State Dominance", in *The Politics of Religion in Indonesia: Syncretism, Orthodoxy, and Religious Contention in Java and Bali*, by Michel Picard and Rémy Madinier (Routledge, 2011), pp. 92–114.

20. "Sydney Jones: ISIS tidak akan berhasil di Indonesia" [Sydney Jones: ISIS will not prevail in Indonesia], Detik.com, 21 August 2014 <http://news.detik.com/read/2014/08/21/103357/2668328/1513/sydney-jones-isis-tidak-akan-berhasil-di-indonesia>.

21. See the latest issue of HTI journal Tabloid *Media Umat*, no. 133, September 2014.

22. Interview with Ismail Yusanto, spokesperson of the HTI, Jakarta, 21 August 2014.

23. With the exception of imprisoned ex-leader of the Jemaah Islamiyah, Abu Bakar Ba'asyir, and part of the Jamaat Anshorut Tauhid (JAT).

24. Telephone interview with Ahmad Najib Burhani, Indonesian Institute of Sciences (LIPI) researcher, 29 August 2014.

25. "RI needs law on hate speech: Activists", TheJakartaPost.com, 5 June 2012 <http://www.thejakartapost.com/news/2012/06/05/ri-needs-law-hate-speech-activists.html>.

16

JOKOWI'S KEY ECONOMIC CHALLENGE
Improving Fiscal Policy for Equitable Growth

Maxensius Tri Sambodo and
Siwage Dharma Negara

INTRODUCTION

Now that he has won the election, Indonesian President-elect Joko "Jokowi" Widodo has only three months in which to prepare and consolidate his actionable economic platform before his inauguration day in October. There remain significant economic challenges awaiting him. Expectations are great that he will lead the country to become a great nation, in a style

Maxensius Tri Sambodo and Siwage Dharma Negara are both Visiting Fellows at ISEAS and researchers at the Economic Research Center at Lembaga Ilmu Pengetahuan Indonesia (LIPI; the Indonesian Institute of Sciences). The authors are grateful for comments and suggestions from Cassey Lee and Ulla Fionna. The usual caveat applies.

similar to his political coalition's name, *Koalisi Indonesia Hebat* (the great Indonesia coalition). He will however need to be realistic in identifying his priorities within his five-year term. Not only will he need to select well the cabinet ministers who will work with him in fulfiling his campaign promises but he will also have to find the money needed to implement many of his development programmes.

Against this backdrop, this essay discusses the fiscal challenges faced by the new government, and argues that improving future fiscal policy is crucial to the achievement of more equitable growth.

THE POLITICAL ECONOMY OF FISCAL SPACE

A key challenge facing Jokowi will be fiscal space. This refers to the availability of government revenues for developmental expenditures. Jokowi will inherit little fiscal space for his own development programmes due to President Susilo Bambang Yudhoyono's (SBY) populist policy on energy subsidies. Between 2009 and 2014, the share of energy subsidies to the total central government spending increased significantly from 7.6 per cent to about 27.4 per cent.[1] In 2014, Indonesia spent about US$33 billion on fuel and electricity subsidies, and ironically, these primarily benefitted the midde class and have long been criticized for being poorly targeted and detrimental to Indonesia's goal to achieve energy security. Worse still, the amount allocated for energy subsidies is higher than central government spending on education, healthcare and social protection programmes. During SBY's second term, energy subsidies grew much higher than central government revenues did. As a result, Indonesia's budget deficit increased from 1.6 per cent of GDP in 2009 to 2.4 per cent of GDP in 2014.

Jokowi is fully aware that the fiscal situation will be critical to his own plans. In his campaign, he promised to develop the country's infrastructure, boost productivity in the agriculture and manufacturing sectors, improve human capital, and provide better healthcare, education and social protection for Indonesians.[2] In particular, in late August 2014, Jokowi requested President SBY to increase fuel prices for fear of an increasing budget deficit due to domestic fuel consumption exceeding the quota in the 2014 state budget. SBY refused, stating that the timing was not right.[3]

There has been some speculation about this refusal to increase fuel prices. First, the budget for 2015 was designed to maintain Indonesia's fiscal balance and to achieve a level of output or service delivery similar to that in 2014. The 2015 budget draft has no allocation for initiative programmes — even the planned ministry expenditure is lower than the medium-term projection (Table 1), and covers only basic or operational costs. However, the non-ministry spending, for debt and subsidy, is increasing above the initial projection, which is a source of worry. Overall, the proposed 2015 state budget is higher than the medium-term projection, due to changes in the macroeconomic assumptions[4] and in government policy including that on energy subsidies. SBY has been using this budget draft to show that his

TABLE 1
Reconciliation of Central Government Spending, 2015 (Rp trillion)

Description	2015 Budget		Gap Description		
	Medium term expenditure projection[a]	Planned expenditure[b]	Nominal	Decomposition $(c) = (d) + (f)$	
				Assumption	Policy
	(a)	(b)	$(c) = (a) - (b)$	(d)	(f)
Ministry	680.3	600.6	(79.7)	0.2	(79.4)
Baseline	612.4	600.6	(11.8)	0.2	(11.5)
Initiative	67.9	—	(67.9)	—	(67.9)
Non Ministry	620.5	779.3	158.8	94.3	64.5
Debt management programme	130.8	154.0	23.2	30.6	(7.4)
Subsidy management programme	339.7	433.5	93.9	66.1	27.8
Total	1,300.7	1,379.9	79.1	94.0	(14.9)

Note: a. Based on the budget projection prepared by the Ministry of Finance and on medium-term planning 2015–2019;
     b. Based on the drafted budget that the government submitted to parliament.
Source: Government Budget 2015.

government wants to keep economic stability through the maintainance of existing subsidies programmes.

Second, SBY's refusal to increase fuel price may be a form of retaliation to previous opposition from the Indonesian Democratic Party – Struggle (PDI-P) to his own plans to increase fuel prices in May 2013. At that time, PDI-P submitted a white paper pressing the SBY government to avoid fuel price increases and instead suggesting that the government try to increase tax revenue, improve spending efficiency and minimize leakage in the budget.[5]

Given SBY's decision to maintain fuel subsidies and leave a small fiscal space for the incoming government, President-elect Jokowi has to consider reducing the amount of subsidy by increasing domestic fuel prices as soon as he takes over the leadership. This will not be an easy move. Jokowi will most likely face strong opposition from a parliament over which his party does not have control. The opposition Red-and-White Coalition under Prabowo now controls 63 per cent of the seats in parliament. Nonetheless, Jokowi may still have an opportunity to implement this change, if what his vice president, Yusuf Kalla, says is true — that the government does not need approval from parliament to increase domestic fuel prices.[6]

Assuming the new government can gradually remove fuel subsidies, the next challenge it faces is to finance infrastructure development, and improve education, healthcare and social protection.[7] Revising budget allocations is possible under the existing budget law. Even though President SBY has proposed the 2015 budget to the parliament (DPR), it is still not a rigid document. The 2015 budget was prepared based on the 2015 government working plan (*Rencana Kerja Pemerintah*, RKP). The latter is designed based on the 2015–19 national medium-term development plan (*Rencana Pembangunan Jangka Menengah Nasional*, RPJMN). The RPJMN will later become an official development guideline after it is signed by the president in early 2015. Given the ongoing process of finalizing the RPJMN, President Jokowi will have the opportunity to revise the 2015 RKP and state budget soon after he approves the 2015–19 RPJMN.

In addition to changing future budget allocations, there are several ways he can consider to increase the fiscal space, including raising tax revenue and improving spending efficiency.[8]

Rising Tax Revenue

As stated in his economic platform, Jokowi promises to increase Indonesia's tax ratio to about 16 per cent by 2019. Indonesia's tax to GDP ratio has increased slightly from 11.2 per cent in 2009 to about 12.2 per cent in 2014. However, the country's tax ratio is relatively low compared to neighbouring countries such as Malaysia (16 per cent), Thailand (15 per cent), Vietnam (21 per cent) and the Philippines (13 per cent).[9] Even Laos, at 15 per cent, has a higher tax ratio than Indonesia.[10] Given the poor taxation system and tax enforcement in the country, increasing the tax ratio will be an uphill battle for the new government even if that is the right direction to take for Indonesia's future fiscal improvement.

Likewise, Jokowi needs to expedite reforms within the Indonesian tax office. Improved performance of that office is the key for improving future tax revenue. Tax revenue has two components, income tax and value added tax (VAT) (Figure 1).[11] While the share of VAT to total tax revenue tends to increase (from 30 per cent in 2004 to 40 per cent in 2014), the share of income tax to total tax revenue has tended to decrease since 2011 (see Figure 1). Going forward, the new administration has to work seriously to increase the number of taxpayers not only from businesses but particularly from middle-upper income individuals.[12] As the number of formal workers increases, the possibility of expanding the number of middle income taxpayers increases in possibility.[13]

Improving Spending Efficiency

Increased tax revenue is not the only way to improve the fiscal situation. Most importantly, the new government must also improve its spending efficiency. This can only be done by improving budget transparency. According to the Corruption Eradication Commission (KPK), most corruption cases related to budget spending are in the form of irregularities on good and services procurement and bribery.[14] In addition, KPK has estimated that between 2010 and 2013, the loss from Indonesia's mining sector due to corrupt practices involving tax officers and mining companies reached Rp50 trillion (US$3.9 billion).[15]

FIGURE 1
Composition of Central Government Revenue

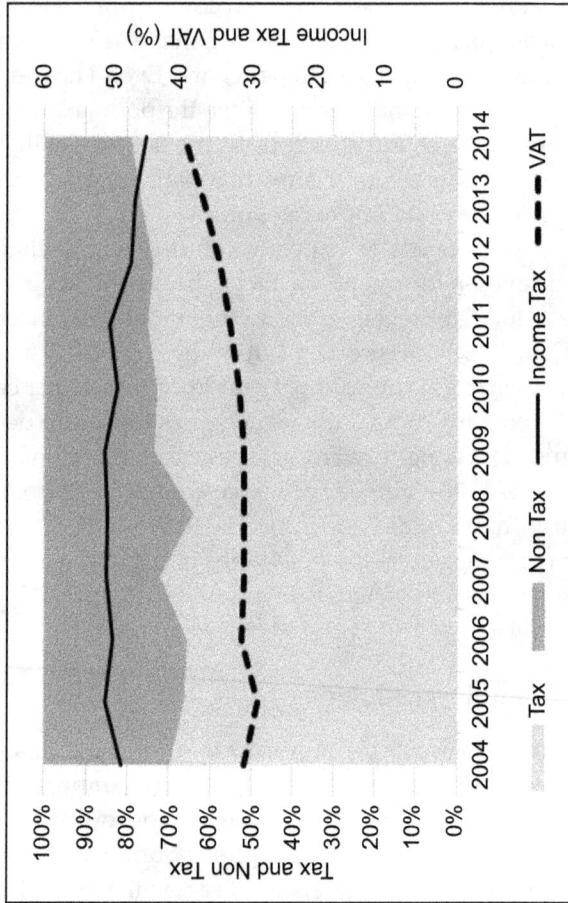

Note: Income tax and VAT as share of tax.
Source: Calculated from various issues of Survey of Recent Development (BIES), Bulletin of Indonesian Economic Studies.

FISCAL POLICY TO IMPROVE GROWTH QUALITY

Indonesia's strong economic growth during SBY era has masked the fact that many have not beneffited from it. During SBY's term in power, the Gini coefficient, measuring income inequality, has indeed worsened (Table 2). The new Jokowi administration will surely need fiscal ammunition to implement policy designed at lowering income inequality, eradicating poverty, improving infrastructure, and promoting education, healthcare and social protection, while maintaining high economic growth to create more jobs for Indonesia's expanding labour market.[16]

A sound fiscal policy will be needed to beef up economic growth especially when the overall growth outlook is looking rather uncertain. In fact, Indonesia's economic growth has been declining since 2011 (see Table 2). This decline has been driven by several external factors, including lower exports revenue due to weakening global commodity prices, China's economic slowdown, and weakening global economic growth. In addition to the external factors, domestic problems such as poor infrastructure, the inefficient logistics sector, the low quality of government spending (too much on fuel subsidy and too little on infrastructure), poor linkages to the global production network, the export ban on unprocessed mining products,

TABLE 2
Economic and Social Indicators, 2009–2014

Indicators	2009	2010	2011	2012	2013	2014
GDP growth (%)	4.5	6.1	6.5	6.23	5.78	5.11
Poverty rate (%)	14.15	12.49	12.36	11.66	11.47	10.96
Number of poor (million)	32.53	30.02	29.89	28.59	28.55	27.73
Gini index	0.37	0.38	0.41	0.41	0.413	n.a
Unemployment (%)	9.26	8.59	8.12	6.24	5.82	5.94
Number of unemployment (million)	8.14	7.41	6.8	7.66	7.2	7.24

Note: GDP growth is up to quarter III/2014; open unemployment 2014 up to August; poverty on September 2014.
Source: Statistics Indonesia, BPS.

and other regulatory restrictions, have made Indonesia's manufacturing sector lose its competitiveness. As a result, the manufacturing output stays stagnant, less jobs are created and eventually the economy suffers from slower economic growth.

A sound fiscal policy can also help Indonesia raise its growth quality. Despite successfully lowering the poverty rate during the SBY term, Indonesia still has not been successful in dealing with unemployment and income inequality (Table 2). The new government will need to use its fiscal policy to build the required fundamentals for generating more inclusive growth. Hill, Khan and Zhuang (2013) argues that to create more inclusive growth, the government must have sufficient resources to (i) maximize economic opportunity; (ii) provide social safety nets; and (iii) ensure equal access to economic opportunity. Clearly, these will need money and good programme implementation.

Jokowi has also promised to prioritize human capital through improving education quality. It is important to note that despite constant increases in the budget allocation to education since 2009, Indonesian students still rank poorly in international tests for mathematics, reading, and science (PISA).[17] Given this poor outcome, the new government should seriously evaluate the effectiveness and transparency of education investment in the country.

The Jokowi administration has also set the goal of improving the quality of health and nutrition of Indonesians. Presently, a high percentage of children in Indonesia are stunted (about 35.6 per cent).[18] This figure is higher than for Myanmar, the Philippines and Vietnam.[19] This trend is worrisome as early childhood health and nutrition is a key determinant for future labour productivity.[20] In order to tackle this problem, the new government will need resources, and food security programmes will be key for providing the country with the required nutrition.

During his campaign, Jokowi proposed scaling up what the Jakarta provincial government has pioneered in the form of free education and health service for the poor. Implementing his education and health card programmes nationwide will required an allocation of Rp40 trillion (US$3.1 billion).[21] It is hoped that reductions in energy subsidies, which can reach Rp70 trillion (US$5.6 billion), will help finance this.[22]

Finally, the new government has to seriously continue the existing social protection plan to ensure that the benefits of economic growth can reach the whole population. Since social assistance and labour market programmes do not reach down to most of the poor today, the new government has to ensure a better targeting mechanism for its social protection programmes.[23] The implementation of future social protection programmes needs to be monitored closely, and be accompanied by full transparency and accountability measures.

CONCLUSION

Jokowi and his new administration should for starters quickly ease fiscal constraints by lowering fuel subsidies. In the medium term, increasing tax revenue and improving public spending efficiency are crucial measures for strengthening future state budget and improving the overall fiscal situation. The fiscal policy for the future needs to be geared toward more productive and long-lasting investments in education, health and infrastructure.

Notes

1. Government budget consists of two elements: (i) central government spending; and (ii) transfer to local government.
2. For detail information on the vision and mission of Jokowi, refer to <http://kpu.go.id/koleksigambar/VISI_MISI_Jokowi-JK.pdf> (accessed 28 August 2014).
3. "Jokowi: SBY tolak naikkan harga BBM" [Jokowi: SBY refuses to increase petroleum price] <http://www.republika.co.id/berita/nasional/politik/14/08/28/nb034i1-jokowi-sby-tolak-naikkan-harga-bbm> (accessed 28 August 2014).
4. The macroeconomic assumptions cover economic growth, inflation, interest rate, oil price and exchange rate.
5. "PDI-P diminta konsisten dalam sikap" [PDI-P asks for consistent in attitude] <http://www.sindotrijaya.com/news/detail/7325/pdip-diminta-konsisten-dalam-sikap#.U_9T5aN-SoE> (accessed 29 August 2014).
6. "Keputusan Kenaikan Harga BBM, JK: Tidak Butuh Persetujuan DPR" [Increasing the price of petrol, JK: Does not need approval from the parliament]

<http://finance.detik.com/read/2014/08/25/185705/2672150/1034/ keputusan-kenaikan-harga-bbm-jk-tidak-butuh-persetujuan-dpr> (accessed 29 August 2014).

7. Heller (2005) pointed out that reprioritizing expenditure refers to the cutting of unproductive spending.

8. According to Heller (2005), fiscal space is "the availability of budgetary room that allows a government to provide resources for a desired purpose without any prejudice to the sustainability of a government's financial position".

9. See McCawley (2014), Table 11.1.

10. Ibid.

11. Tax consists of domestic tax (income tax, Value Added Tax, and other) and international trade taxes. Non-tax consists of natural-resource revenues, profits of state owned enterprises, revenue from public-service centres, and other

12. See Gunawan and Siregar (2009).

13. In August 2008, 31 per cent of employee worked in the formal sector, while in February 2014, about 40.9 per cent of employee were in formal sector (information obtain from <http://www.bps.go.id/brs_file/naker_05mei14. pdf> and <http://www.bps.go.id/brs_file/naker-05jan09.pdf?>).

14. KPK's annual report (various years).

15. "KPK: Potensi Kerugian Negara di Sektor Minerba Mencapai Rp 50 triliun" [KPK: Potential loss from the mining sector reached IDR 50 trillion] <http:// nasional.kompas.com/read/2014/05/23/2051174/KPK.Potensi.Kerugian. Negara.di.Sektor.Minerba.Mencapai.Rp.50.Triliun> (accessed 29 August 2014).

16. Refer to <http://www.iseas.edu.sg/documents/publication/ISEAS_ Perspective_2014_40.pdf> for a detailed discussion on Joko Widodo's economic platform.

17. See <http://www.oecd.org/pisa/keyfindings/pisa-2012-results-overview.pdf> (accessed 25 July 2014).

18. See UNICEF (2014). "The State of the World's Children 2014". New York <http://www.unicef.org/sowc2013/> (accessed 25 July 2014).

19. Ibid.

20. See Coxhead (2014) for detailed discussions.

21. <http://pemilu.tempo.co/read/news/2014/06/15/269585239/Debat-Capres-Jokowi-Pertahankan-Wajib-Belajar>.

22. Ibid.

23. See ADB (2013).

References

Asian Development Bank (ADB). *The Social Protection Index: Assessing Results for Asia and the Pacific*. Manila: ADB, 2013.

Coxhead, I. "Indonesia: returns to occupation, education, and ability during a resource export boom". In *Trade, Development, and Political Economy in East Asia*, edited by P. Authukorala, A.A. Patunru and B.P. Resosudarmo (Singapore: Institute of Southeast Asian Studies, 2014).

Gunawan, A., and Siregar, R. "Survey of Recent Development". *Bulletin of Indonesian Economic Studies* 45, no. 1 (2009): 9–38.

Heller, P.S. "Understanding Fiscal Space". *IMF Policy Discussion Paper*, PDP 05/4, March 2005.

Hill, H., M.E. Khan and J. Zhuang. "Introduction". In *Diagnosing the Indonesian Economy: Toward Inclusive and Green Growth*, edited by H. Hill, M.E. Khan and J. Zhuang. Manila: ADB, 2013.

McCawley, P. "Rethinking the role of the state in ASEAN". In, *Trade, Development, and Political Economy in East Asia*, edited by P. Authukorala, A.A. Patunru and B.P. Resosudarmo (Singapore: Institute of Southeast Asian Studies, 2014).

World Bank. "Development Policy Review: Indonesia Avoiding the Trap", 2014 <http://www.worldbank.org/en/news/feature/2014/06/23/indonesia-2014-development-policy-review> (accessed 20 July 2014).

17

CROSSING THE RIVER
WHILE AVOIDING THE STONES
Jokowi's Run-up to the Presidency

Ulla Fionna and Francis E. Hutchinson

INTRODUCTION

Karl Marx famously said that men make their own history, but not under circumstances that they choose. Rather, they must act within existing circumstances that are "transmitted from the past". Joko Widodo (Jokowi) represents a new breed of Indonesian politicians, and is in fact a creation arising from the newly decentralized polity of the post- Suharto period. Despite this new situation, Jokowi must act within a complex political and institutional context. And, in the coming few weeks before he assumes office, several of the institutional junctures that Indonesia will traverse are

Ulla Fionna is Fellow at ISEAS and **Francis Hutchinson** is Senior Fellow at ISEAS. This article was prepared before the plenary meeting on the regional elections (Pilkida) bill at the House of Representatives (DPR) on 25 September 2014. It was first published on 29 September 2014 as *ISEAS Perspective* 2014/49.

not within his control. The sum of these events will largely determine the effectiveness of his administration.

THE ROAD TO THE PRESIDENCY

In July 2014, Joko Widodo faced off against Prabowo Subianto in the Indonesian presidential election. Touted as the most polarizing presidential election that the country has ever seen, the close and fiercely contested race pitted a member of the country's old political elite against someone new and fresh, but with solid administrative credentials. Jokowi started as a small business owner from the town of Solo (Central Java), and went on to become Mayor of that city and then Governor of Jakarta. Prabowo, in contrast, comes from a line of technocrats and had a successful career in the military before turning to politics.[1] After an intense campaign and election, the General Election Commission announced that Jokowi had won 53.15 per cent of votes against Prabowo's 46.85 per cent on 22 July.

Alleging vote-rigging and fraud, the Prabowo camp decided to contest the elections before the Constitutional Court. In August, following a short and succinct review of the plaintiff's complaints however, the Court rejected his requests to cancel Jokowi's victory and conduct a re-vote. While Prabowo has yet to officially concede defeat, influential members of his coalition — including Hashim Djojohadikusumo, his brother, and Hatta Rajasa, his vice-presidential candidate and leader of PAN — have acknowledged Jokowi's victory.

Jokowi's presidency will mark the first time since Indonesia's independence that a locally elected politician assumes national office. However, despite his personal popularity, political capital, and goodwill, Jokowi will have to manoeuvre a number of key tests that will determine the course and impact of his office.

THE TRANSITION

While Jokowi may be riding a wave of considerable momentum, he will need to use his political capital wisely. One of his first priorities will be to reduce the budget-sapping fuel subsidy, a historically tense political issue that has largely underwritten the transport costs of the upper and middle classes. This may mean that he will have no fiscal space to move on his health and education pledges. Moreover, his requests for a transition budget — jointly formulated with SBY — were rebuffed. This could be due to a combination of factors, ranging from the outgoing President's desire to protect his legacy to an unwillingness to aid a political *parvenu* of Jokowi's kind. Indeed, the one-to-one meeting between the two men to discuss transition issues lasted considerably longer than anticipated, mainly due to their inability to reach an agreement on this issue.

The next critical test was on 25 September 2014 when the House of Representatives would vote on whether to retain or discard the direct election of mayors and regency heads in favour of indirect elections. The latter choice, favoured by the old political elite, would see regional legislatures directly elected as in the past, but choosing mayors or regency heads from among their own ranks. The current formula, in use since 2005, has been criticized for servicing money politics. In addition, the elimination of direct elections for public office would curtail the ability of new leaders to emerge. Beyond Jokowi, direct elections have enabled capable local-level leaders such as Ridwan Kamil, the mayor of Bandung, and Tri Rismaharini, the mayor of Surabaya, to attain office through direct appeals to the electorate.

While really a bell-wether of SBY's democratic credentials as opposed to Jokowi's, this impending decision will dramatically affect the political context within which the new President must manoeuvre. A reversal would dramatically favour the old elite, who would be better placed to lobby current legislators to appoint members from their ranks. It would mean dealing with not just the House of Representatives, but also with legions of local leaders — the majority of which would be from the old political elite.

At present, Jokowi does not have enough support in the national parliament to block this proposal. Despite him being media savvy and public opinion — which is largely in favour of retaining the status quo — being in his favour, the decision will be made by sitting legislators who are beholden to their party leaders. However, SBY's Democrat Party could tip the balance. While the President has stated his support for direct elections, his party only declared its support on 18 September. On the one hand, this is in line with SBY's public position. But, on the other, it means going against the large and influential Merah-Putih coalition led by Prabowo.[2]

WEAPONS OF THE WILFUL

While the broader political context within which he will govern is beyond his control, Jokowi can move on two fronts to bolster his position. The first of these is his coalition in parliament. As it stands, Jokowi's coalition comprises a mere 37 per cent of the 560 member parliament.[3] In contrast, Prabowo's Merah-Putih coalition brings together the other 63 per cent.[4]

An opposition coalition of this magnitude constitutes a major structural constraint. As it stands, Prabowo's Merah-Putih coalition may well attempt to impeach Jokowi in the first parliamentary sitting if he attempts to reduce the fuel subsidies. The opposition has alleged that eliminating or reducing the subsidy would entail a major economic burden for average Indonesians and would constitute a violation of the constitution. This is due to Article 33, which states that it is the government's responsibility to manage natural resources for the greatest public benefit.

That said, given the privileges of office, observers have predicted that the opposition coalition would crumble. As it is, there are factions in two smaller parties, the United Development Party (PPP) and the National Mandate Party (PAN), that are allegedly in favour of crossing the floor. PAN, a Muslim-based nationalist party, is a middle-sized party which managed sixth place this year at the parliamentary elections. This issue is currently being debated at the highest levels in the party. While party founder Amien Rais is adamant in his support for Prabowo, Hatta Rajasa, Prabowo's vice-presidential candidate, is seen to be leaning towards the government coalition.

PPP is one of Indonesia's most established political parties. Nominally Islamist, it was one of only three parties allowed to compete under the New Order, and even had former president Suharto as its chairman for a short period. In post-1998 Indonesia, it was steadily losing votes until this year, which saw it recover slightly to rank ninth in the votes garnered. The PPP has publicly maintained its commitment to eliminating direct elections, even under its new, more democratically-oriented leadership. However, there is strong grass-roots support for retaining the current political structure. The PPP's former chairman Suryadharma Ali — recently detained on corruption charges — faced strong protests within his party when he made a public appearance at a rally organized by

Prabowo's party, Gerindra. Thus, a last minute turnaround cannot be completely ruled out.

Despite its close alliance with Prabowo during the election, it is even conceivable that Golkar may cross the floor. Party Chairman Aburizal Bakrie's decision to side with Prabowo has proven unpopular among party officials, even leading some to call for his replacement. And it should not be forgotten that Joko's Vice-President, Jusuf Kalla, also retains considerable influence within the party. However, the hold of Akbar Tandjung — a prominent party member and former minister under the New Order — on Golkar, and his close relationship with Prabowo may tilt the balance towards the Merah-Putih coalition.

An inter-linked challenge for Jokowi is the composition of his cabinet. He has been adamant that positions would not be allocated in return for support for his coalition. Instead, Jokowi has opted for a different approach in allocating appointments. His team has set up a website with the names of potential candidates for each ministerial post. This has been well-received by the public.[5] This is consistent with his term as governor of Jakarta, when he adopted "open selection"[6] for the positions of *camat* (sub-district leaders) and *lurah* (village heads).

However, despite Jokowi's promise to establish a skinny (*ramping*) cabinet, he has announced that he will have thirty-four ministerial positions — similar to the number under SBY's administration, and more than initially indicated. He has announced that over half of his cabinet (eighteen) will be technocrats, including the ministers of finance, energy and state-owned enterprises. Jokowi's team said that the remaining sixteen positions could be filled by members of various parties, but candidates are still required to have relevant expertise.[7]

A transitional team has been set up to prepare for Jokowi's inauguration. The reactions have been mixed as he has already been criticized for the appointment of Rini Soemarno as its head. As the former minister of trade and industry, Soemarno is a close aide of Megawati, the former president and current chair of Jokowi's party, PDI-P. During her tenure as minister, Soemarno implemented a number of politically unpopular protectionist policies and was allegedly involved in a few high-profile corruption scandals.[8]

Furthermore, her links with Megawati raise questions over the extent to which Jokowi will be independent. There have also been criticisms over the choice of former National Intelligence Agency Gen. (ret) A.M. Hendropriyono as an advisor to the team. Hendropriyono has been allegedly involved in human rights abuse cases.[9] Beyond the specifics of these allegations, it is also imperative for Jokowi to reach out to Indonesia's powerful military.

The fact that no parties from the opposing coalition have yet crossed the floor could mean that they are holding out for more choice appointments to be made available. However, the size and composition of Jokowi's first cabinet will be a key indicator of his tenure. If too many key appointments are given to party insiders, he will lose legitimacy. And if he does not succeed in enticing more parties to join his coalition, Jokowi will face opposition for every significant measure.

The inevitable horse-trading has taken longer than anticipated, meaning that Jokowi may well either declare his cabinet line-up only just before his inauguration, or immediately after. If the latter, he would have reneged on his pledge to unveil his line-up before assuming office. However, more than the timing, the composition of the cabinet will determine the stock of political capital Jokowi will possess upon assuming the Presidency.

CONCLUSION

The next few weeks will be vital for Jokowi's presidency. In the wider context, he has no control over whether direct elections will be retained. If they are retained, the traditional elite will be occupied with attempting to retain the vestiges of their influence at the local level. If they are not, he will be the product of an all-too-brief experiment with grass-roots democracy and the vertical mobility it offered to non-traditional politicians.

Regardless of this, Jokowi will have to move quickly and invest his political capital wisely. Policy priority number one is to reduce the fuel subsidies to create the financial wherewithal needed for him to invest in health and education initiatives. Beyond the measure itself, Jokowi will need to be backed up by a solid team and a somewhat larger parliamentary faction. Despite their mutually exclusive nature, the upcoming president will have to achieve moderate success in both these tests. Most presidencies are given a grace period of 100 days in office. Jokowi must be acutely aware that his 100 days have already started.

Notes

1. Prabowo's grandfather Margono Djojohadikusumo was one of the founders of Bank Negara Indonesia (Indonesian State Bank). He also led the Provisional Advisory Council (Dewan Pertimbangan Agung Sementara) and the Committee for Preparatory Work for Indonesian Independence (Badan Penyelidik Usaha Persiapan Kemerdekaan Indonesia, BPUPKI). Prabowo's father Soemitro Djojohadikusumo was a prominent economist, who served as minister for the economy and for research and technology.

2. Moch Harun Syah, "Partai Demokrat Dukung Pilkada Langsung" [Democratic Party Supports Direct Election for Local Leaders], *liputan6news* <http://news. liputan6.com/read/2106882/partai-demokrat-dukung-pilkada-langsung> (accessed 19 September 2014).

3. Joining Jokowi's Indonesian Democratic Party – Struggle (Partai Demokrasi Indonesia, PDI-P) are the following: National Awakening Party (Partai Kebangkitan Bangsa, PKB); National Democratic Party (Partai Nasdem, Partai Nasional Demokrat); People's Conscience Party (Partai Hanura, Partai Hati Nurani Rakyat); and Indonesian Justice and Unity Party (Partai Keadilan dan Persatuan Indonesia, PKPI).

4. Joining Gerindra in Prabowo's coalition are these parties: National Mandate Party (Partai Amanat Nasional, PAN), United Development Party (Partai Persatuan Pembangunan, PPP), Prosperous Justice Party (Partai Keadilan Sejahtera, PKS), Crescent Star Party (Partai Bulan Bintang, PBB), Democratic Party (Partai Demokrat, PD), and Golkar Party (Partai Golkar, Functional Group Party).

5. The first stage of polling is now closed and results can be found here <http://www.jokowicenter.com/2014/08/pers-rilis-hasil-polling-menteri-kaur-tahap-i/> and the second stage can be found here <http://www.jokowicenter.com/polling-menteri/>.

6. This is a fit and proper test, where every candidate who meets requirements may submit proposals of a plan of what he/she intends to do if selected. The provincial government deliberates and announces the results and decides on the placement, and also assess the success and efficiency of the selected candidate.

7. "Indonesia's president-elect Widodo looks to technocrat for cabinet", reuters, 15 September 2014 <http://uk.reuters.com/article/2014/09/15/uk-indonesia-politics-idUKKBN0HA16I20140915> (accessed 19 September 2014).
8. "Rini Soemarno Dianggap Ancaman Bagi Jokowi" [Rini Soemarno Considered as Threat for Jokowi], *tribunnews.com*, 6 August 2014 <http://www.tribunnews.com/nasional/2014/08/06/rini-soemarno-dianggap-ancaman-bagi-jokowi> (accessed 19 August 2014).
9. Haeril Halim and Margareth S. Aritonang, "Controversial Hendropriyono gets transition team support", *Jakarta Post*, 11 August 2014 <http://www.thejakartapost.com/news/2014/08/11/controversial-hendropriyono-gets-transition-team-support.html> (accessed 20 August 2014).

18

POST-ELECTIONS INDONESIA
Towards a Crisis of Government?

Max Lane

INTRODUCTION

On 25 September 2014, the Indonesian People's Representative Council (Dewan Perwakilan Rakyat, DPR) passed legislation ending the direct election of governors, *bupati* (regent/district head) and mayors. This new legislation returns the electoral process for these positions to that which was employed during the New Order period and until 2004. Under this old-new process, the municipal, district and provincial legislative councils (Dewan Perwakilan Rakyat Daerah, DPRD) will be the ones voting for these positions. The results of the vote will then be sent to the President, who will then appoint these officials. Significantly, the positions of *bupati* and mayor have become much more important over the last ten years as

Max Lane is Visiting Fellow at ISEAS, Lecturer in Southeast Asian politics and history at Victoria University, and Honorary Associate in Indonesian Studies at the University of Sydney. This article was first published on 16 October 2014 as *ISEAS Perspective* 2014/53.

a result of the various decentralization laws, which allocate substantial budgetary powers to the legislative councils and administrations at the municipal and district levels.

The passing of this law was the result of an assertive campaign in parliament by the Red and White Coalition (Koalisi Merah Putih, KMP), comprising of the parties that nominated Prabowo Subianto as candidate in the recent presidential election.[1] In the election, Subianto lost by a narrow margin to Joko Widodo — 47 per cent to 53 per cent, a difference of 8 million votes out of 190 million. Subianto was nominated by his own party, Gerindra, Golkar, the Prosperous Justice Party (Partai Keadilan Sejahtera, PKS), the National Mandate Party (Partai Amanat Nasional, PAN) and United Development Party (Partai Persatuan Pembangunan, PPP). Widodo was nominated by the Indonesian Democratic Party – Struggle (Partai Demokrasi Indonesia Perjuangan, PDI-P), the Nasional Democratic Party (Nasdem), the National Awakening Party (Partai Kebangkitan Bangsa, PKB), the Peoples' Conscience Party (Partai Hati Nurani Rakyat, Hanura) and the Unity and Justice Party of Indonesia (Partai Keadilan dan Persatuan Indonesia, PKPI). The passing of the law will very likely deliver governor positions to KMP nominees in thirty-one out of thirty-four provinces.[2] Should this come about, it would provide an additional strong platform from which the KMP can oppose the Widodo–PDI-P–led government and try to implement its own policy agenda.

Another party with a substantial number of seats is the Democratic Party (Partai Demokrat, PD), headed by incumbent President Yudhoyono. Most of the PD members walked out during the vote for the bill, effectively abstaining, which gave the KMP a majority in the parliament. President Yudhoyono was overseas at the time and in recent statements seems to be trying to create the impression that the walk-out was not supposed to happen. He initially hinted that he would not sign the bill into law. Under the Indonesian system, a law should be both passed by the DPR and signed by the President before it takes effect. However, it will still come into effect after thirty days even without the President's signature. On 2 October, Yudhoyono did sign off on the new legislation but at the same time, he issued two Presidential Regulations that would annul the new law and reinstate direct elections.[3] These Presidential Regulations would however require the support of a majority in the new parliament to be implemented.[4] However, the PD siding with the Widodo–PDI-P–led coalition would provide only 48 per cent of the seats, which is insufficient to confirm the regulations.[5] The PDI-P–led coalition combined with the PD would have 268 seats to the KMP's 273. While a PDI-P–PD voting bloc is not impossible, the fact that the PD voted as a bloc with the KMP parties to elect the chairman and vice- chairmen of the DPR, excluding any representative from the PDI-P coalition, indicates that the PD may demand something substantial to side with the PDIP coalition.[6]

President-elect Joko Widodo indicated in the national TV debates with Prabowo that he supported the current system of direct elections, as did his party, the PDI-P.[7] This is also the position of Vice-President-elect, Jusuf Kalla, although in the past he had supported a return to the old system.[8] The PDI-P has said it will take the matter to the Constitutional Court, at the same time indicating that it will accept the Court's ruling on the issue even if it were in favour of the legislation.[9] PDI-P's coalition partner, the Nasdem, has also specified that it would accept the Constitutional Court's decision.[10]

TWO ELECTIONS, TWO RESULTS

The present impasse came about due to the fact that the two elections held this year in Indonesia had different outcomes. The April General Elections revealed a low level of support for the PDI-P, despite the PDI-P announcing just before the campaign that they had selected the popular Joko Widodo as their presidential candidate. A weak campaign by both Widodo and the PDI-P, advocating no clear policies nor establishing a clear, differentiated "political personality", gave the PDI-P only 19 per cent of the votes. This was no doubt bigger than for any other party,[11] but the elections left no party with majority or even near-majority support. At the same time, voter absenteeism was high, with 40 per cent of registered voters not bothering to vote for any party.

This outcome has created a new parliament not too different from the previous one, where the PDI-P is a small minority. The coalition of the PDI-P, Nasdem, PKB and Hanura comprises 37 per cent of parliamentary seats, with the PDI-P having only 19 per cent, or half of this coalition's seats. This coalition will continue to fall short of a majority unless one or more parties from the KMP switch over. Yudhoyono's PD has been the biggest loser and will have a much smaller, but still substantial number of seats, in parliament. As noted above, even if PD supports the Widodo coalition, the KMP would still have a majority, albeit a much slimmer one.[12]

The majority that the election gave the KMP (as long as the coalition stays together) has no doubt provided the KMP with the confidence to adopt a position of outright opposition to Widodo and the PDI-P–led coalition. Although Widodo managed to win the presidency with 53 per cent of the votes, which was 16 per cent above the combined vote-share of the parties that nominated him for the presidency, this was below the more than 60 per cent support rate that he had from earlier opinion polls. Under the circumstances, Widodo appears to be the winner of a "draw".[13]

The presidential election campaign exposed a divide that has been evolving among Indonesia's political elite. This rift is represented on opposing sides by conglomerate capital (the Prabowo Subianto camp), and provincial or district capital (the Joko Widodo camp). Both include conglomerate and local capital, no doubt, but their leading forces are different, which provides the basis for their differing political perspectives. Conglomerate capital proposes a reversion to centralized state power and the promotion of large-scale economic projects.[14] The Widodo–PDI-P–led coalition is comfortable with decentralized capitalism, where there is greater scope for the growth of small and medium-sized capital in the provinces. This split will continue to play out in the contest between the KMP and the Widodo–PDI-P coalition.

THE POLITICAL DIVIDE AND ELECTORAL POLITICS

The KMP coalition is, however, not only motivated by a desire to establish a centralized political system and restore the state-crony axis in the economy. It is also reacting against an inevitable consequence of the establishment of a system where control over the executive government and executive positions depends on winning votes for those positions in direct elections. They need candidates that can win in popularity contests.[15]

Local elite figures have more intimate and real experience in relating to the non-elite population than the big ex-cronies based in Jakarta, who live in elite neighbourhoods and mix among the super-rich. While the vast majority of local leaders emerging out of decentralized capitalism has quickly indulged in local cronyism and corruption, a few have emerged who understand the necessity of winning popularity based on policy delivery, or the image of policy delivery, of whom Widodo is the most outstanding example. During the New Order, the politician's goal was to instil fear and awe, not win popularity, whether by proposing good policies or by lying, cheating and acting. While Prabowo campaigned hard as an electioneering politician, as did Bakrie of Golkar in the April elections, neither prefers it as a political method. Widodo is much more able to stand for two hours shaking poor people's hands than Bakrie or Prabowo, whose style is to exude authority and power. One campaigns using folksy tactics, the other using "strong leader" imagery. But the strong leader, in the end, resents the need to seek consent from those he is supposed to govern.

This new factor — the need to win popularity — has introduced the possibility, indeed the reality of an "anomaly" in the electoral process: a figure from a party or coalition with minority support in parliament can win the highest political office in the nation. The 2014 presidential elections has shown that this is possible, and it could happen at the local level as well.

Thus the KMP, now having passed the legislation abolishing direct elections for regional leaders, is discussing doing the same for the office of the President,[16] intending to return that right to the Peoples' Consultative Assembly (Majelis Permusyawaratan Rakyat, MPR), which is composed of members of the DPR and the Regional Representative Council (Dewan Perwakilan Daerah, DPD).

SUPPORT FOR DIRECT ELECTIONS

Prabowo made it clear during the presidential election campaign that he supported ending direct elections for *bupati*, mayors and governors. On the other hand, Widodo and running mate Kalla defended direct elections, explaining that they would try to save money in its implementation by scheduling all such elections at the same time.

Since the successful move to scrape direct elections by the KMP, there have been widespread statements of support for keeping direct elections for regional leaders. The liberal media, such as *Jakarta Post*, *Jakarta Globe* and *Tempo* newspaper and magazine, have campaigned strongly for a return to direct elections, condemning the KMP for wanting to return to the New Order era.

Statements of support for direct elections have also come from several current *bupati*, mayors and governors. The most publicized and dramatic of these is that of the Deputy Governor of Jakarta, Basuki Tjahaja Purnama (Ahok), who resigned from Prabowo's Gerindra party in protest. The Mayor of Bandung, Ridwan Kamil, who is also head of the All-Indonesia Association of Town Governments (Asosiasi Pemerintah Kota Seluruh Indonesia, Apeksi), has also opposed the move away from direct elections.[17] Kamil was also nominated by Gerindra and another KMP party, the PKS, when standing for election as Mayor.

Outside of this elite-based opposition, there has been a small but increasing number of street protests, either by student or human rights groups, as well as internet-based protests. Twitter protests against PD's abstention reached over 100,000 within a matter of days.[18] This appears to be widespread sentiment. The Indonesian Survey Circle (Lingkaran Survei Indonesia, LSI) revealed that in a poll in September, 81 per cent of respondents supported direct elections of regional leaders, 11 per cent favoured selection by the DPRDs, and 5 per cent supported appointment by the President.[19] Another LSI poll stated that as much as 70 per cent of voters supporting KMP parties supported President Yudhoyono's decision to issue presidential regulations that sought to reinstate direct elections.[20]

It is likely that new coalitions of human rights, student and other "civil society" organizations will emerge to campaign for the restoration of direct elections. However, how far such a movement can grow will, to some extent, be dependent on the direct leadership and support of Widodo and the PDI-P.

Since the presidential election, there has been enormous speculation, especially in the media sympathetic to Widodo, that one or more of the parties in the KMP would cross over to the Widodo–PDI-P camp. Every non-appearance of a KMP figure at a KMP event now creates a flurry of speculation. This has been fuelled by public statements from some figures in Golkar, PPP and PAN that they would prefer to be in government with Widodo and the PDI-P. However, up until September 2014, no such cross-over has yet happened, although it is clear that Widodo and the PDI-P have been encouraging this possibility. Both Widodo and Megawati regularly make statements encouraging other parties to join their coalition, and efforts have been made by PDI-P to win over PPP, PAN and PD. PDI-P spokespersons have also stated publicly that they have decided against mass mobilization, preferring instead to confine their actions to formal legal channels.[21] If this position changes, there may be a chance to garner and bring to the fore public support for direct elections as reflected in social media, street actions and public opinion polls.

The election of a Golkar politician as chairman of the DPR, and Gerindra, PKS and PAN members as vice-chairmen, to the exclusion of any representative from the PDI-P–led coalition, indicates that this lobbying has been unsuccessful so far. This was possible after KMP's earlier triumph in changing the old rule that automatically gave the DPR chairman position to the party that won the most seats, which would have been the PDI-P. The new rules opened up all positions to a majority vote in the DPR, which in this case privileged members of the KMP. In a recent comment, Widodo seems to still hold out hope of winning other parties over.[22] However, in the same statement he warned of potential turbulence in parliament and even claimed that the KMP might attempt to prevent his inauguration on 20 October.[23] If this happens, Indonesia will be without a President, and it would provoke a constitutional crisis where the mechanisms for resolution are unclear. However, such an action by the KMP would contradict a statement made by the coalition's secretary-generals immediately after the Constitutional Court rejected Prabowo's appeal against the election results. In that statement, they accepted the legality of the Constitutional Court's decision, although Gerindra spokespersons still criticize it as unjust.[24]

RULING FROM PARLIAMENT: CHALLENGE OR BARGAINING CHIP?

The KMP has not succeeded only in changing the rules of parliament that resulted in them taking all key parliamentary positions. In addition, it has also returned the power to elect regional leaders to the local legislative councils, and voiced its intention to return the power of electing the President to the MPR.[25] In fact, Prabowo had announced this intention during his election campaign.[26] Should the KMP maintain a clear majority in parliament, the electoral laws could be amended to allow this. The KMP announced that they will set up a parliamentary commission to investigate alleged irregularities in the Election Commission's implementation of the presidential election, opening up the possibility of delegitimizing the results. This would be a more suitable tactic for the KMP to remove Widodo under current laws. The option of impeachment would require politically credible proof of corruption or criminal behavior on the part of Widodo and, in any case, would deliver the presidency to Jusuf Kalla.

More significantly, in the short-term, the KMP plans to change as many as 122 laws, including those covering many areas of the economy, such as banking and telecommunications. Given their numbers in parliament and their control over the positions that manage the parliamentary process, they should be able to set the agenda in accordance with their priorities. This effectively allows them the option to "govern" the country from parliament, and counter the influence of the president. As both can claim electoral legitimacy, based on the two different elections, this may lead to a political crisis at some point.

Another interpretation of the current parliamentary dynamics is that there is still a chance that parties such as the PPP, PAN or PD may join the Widodo–PDI-P coalition, and that their support for the latest maneuvers by the KMP is a tactic for enhancing their bargaining position with the PDI-P. They are making it clear, so the speculation goes, that it would be better for Widodo to give them the necessary ministerial and other positions in exchange for a majority position in parliament and consequently, government stability for the next five years.

If the Widodo–PDI-P coalition fails to win a majority position in parliament, then they should expect constant challenges to the Widodo presidency, and the prospect of a crisis of government is heightened. One of the first tests will be the rectification of Yudhoyono's Presidential Regulations annulling the recently passed election law and reinstating direct elections for regional leaders. The question is also whether public sentiments for retaining direct elections can be mobilized and transformed into a political force that can influence the processes of parliament.

Notes

1. It must be noted, however, that it was the Yudhoyono government's Ministry of Home Affairs that originally proposed this bill. However, after proposing the bill, the government has vacillated many times on the issue.
2. <http://www.tempo.co/read/news/2014/09/08/078605241/UU-Pilkada-Sah-Koalisi-Prabowo-Borong-31-Gubernur>.
3. <http://www.tribunnews.com/nasional/2014/10/02/sby-resmi-tandatangani-dua-perpu-pilkada>; "Indonesian president suspends law scrapping direct regional elections" <http://english.kyodonews.jp/news/2014/10/315253.html>.
4. Yudhoyono has recently claimed he has won support from KMP parties, although he could not say that he had spoken to KMP party leaders <http://nasional.kontan.co.id/news/sby-yakin-dua-perppu-akan-didukung-koalisi-prabowo>.
5. See <http://www.thejakartapost.com/news/2014/10/02/fate-perppu-remains-uncertain.html>.
6. <http://www.smh.com.au/world/joko-widodo-faces-uphill-battle-as-opponents-secure-key-positions-in-indonesias-parliament-20141002-10pe6j.html>.
7. For a recording of this debate, see <https://www.youtube.com/watch?v=MuL-1sW5b-8>. Interestingly, in this debate, Prabowo's Vice-Presidential running mate, Hatta Rajasa, stated a position supporting direct elections but with synchronized local elections throughout the nation.
8. See this 2011 news report <http://www.republika.co.id/berita/nasional/umum/11/10/02/lses3b-jenjang-demokrasi-terlalu-panjang-jk-dukung-pilgub-langsung-dihapus>.
9. <http://news.liputan6.com/read/2111162/jika-tidak-dikabulkan-mk-pdip-akan-bangun-monumen-uu-pilkada>. There have also been media reports quoting some PDI-P officials as stating they have not taken a final decision to take the new law to the Constitutional Court.
10. <http://www.tribunnews.com/nasional/2014/10/01/surya-paloh-sedih-sby-keluarkan-perppu-pilkada>.
11. See Max Lane, "Gap Narrows between Candidates in Indonesian Presidential Elections", *ISEAS Perspective* 2014 #39, 4 July 2014.
12. There appears now also to be the possibility — albeit slim — of the PKB joining the KMP coalition <http://www.republika.co.id/berita/nasional/politik/14/10/01/ncrcp2-tak-diajak-jokowijk-pkb-siap-gabung-koalisi-merah-putih>.

13. This reflects a situation observed in earlier issues of *ISEAS Perspective* emphasizing the low level of support for all parties. It is this situation which allows for the contradiction of a candidate nominated by a party with low popularity, but with popularity beyond the party, winning votes from parties with even lower levels of support. See Max Lane, "Indonesia's 2014 Legislative Elections: The Dilemmas of 'Elektabilitas' Politics", *ISEAS Perspective*, 2014 #25, 23 April 2014.

14. See Max Lane, *Decentralization and Its Discontents: An Essay on Class, Political Agency and National Perspective in Indonesian Politics* (Singapore: Institute of Southeast Asian Studies, 2014), for more on this division.

15. There is little doubt that there is enormous resentment among the figures emerging out of the New Order, and who are based on conglomerate economic power, that they have to compete against a "nobody", i.e. a local merchant from a medium-sized town, who can hardly articulate policies clearly, but somehow can establish a sentimental link with a significant portion of the electorate.

16. <http://thejakartaglobe.beritasatu.com/news/prabowos-coalition-now-gunning-regions-mpr/>; <http://www.thejakartapost.com/news/2014/10/02/fate-perppu-remains-uncertain.html>.

17. <http://regional.kompas.com/read/2014/09/26/17195971/Ridwan.Kamil.Apeksi.Cari.Pengacara.tetapi.Enggak.Bakal.Pakai.Farhat.Abbas>. See also "Across indonesia, local chiefs slam plan to stop all direct polls", *Jakarta Globe*, 7 September 2014.

18. <http://www.thejakartapost.com/news/2014/10/02/beyond-hashtags-netizens-outrage-and-hope.html>; <http://www.thejakartapost.com/news/2014/09/26/shameonyousby-gives-yudhoyono-worldwide-spotlight.html>.

19. <http://thejakartaglobe.beritasatu.com/news/democrats-key-regional-elections-bill/>.

20. <http://intisari-online.com/read/survei-lsi-6992-persen-pemilih-prabowo-hatta-mendukung-sby-keluarkan-perppu-terkait-uu-pilkada>.

21. <http://indonesiasatu.kompas.com/read/2014/10/04/15273911/jika.mau.pdi-p.klaim.bisa.kerahkan.1.juta.orang.untuk.hadang.koalisi.merah.putih>.

22. <http://www.thejakartapost.com/news/2014/10/03/jokowi-strike-back-rivals.html>

23. The parliamentary leadership would have to sign off on the Indonesian Election Commission's report confirming Widodo and Kalla's election victory.

24. <http://nasional.kompas.com/read/2014/08/21/21385001/Koalisi.Merah.Putih.Akui.Putusan.MK.sebagai.Hasil.Akhir.Pilpres>.

25. <http://www.tribunnews.com/nasional/2014/10/03/pdip-curigai-pemilihan-presiden-hendak-dikembalikan-ke-mpr>.
26. Edward Aspinall and Marcus Mietzner, "Prabowo Subianto: Vote for me, but just the once" <http://asiapacific.anu.edu.au/newmandala/2014/06/30/prabowo-subianto-vote-for-me-but-just-the-once/>.

EPILOGUE

JOKOWI'S FIRST MONTHS
Compromise Cabinet, Subsidy Cuts, and Corrupt Coalition

Ulla Fionna

INTRODUCTION: THE VERY SHORT HONEYMOON

Burdened with high expectations on deliverables, Indonesian President Jokowi's first few months have been hectic. The most difficult challenges anticipated at the start of his administration were: whether the cabinet would be dominated by professionals as promised; resistance from the parliamentary opposition; and his plan for an unpopular fuel price hike. Doubts about his choice of cabinet ministers have been mitigated by the hard work that some have demonstrated. Still, his choices for the chiefs of legal and judicial institutions have been met with criticism, and have raised questions about his commitment to clean government and to the combatting of corruption. Meanwhile, fortune has been on his side as the drop in crude oil prices has made the elimination of costly oil subsidies much easier. However, all these seem to be negated by the glaring fact that

Ulla Fionna is Fellow at ISEAS. This article was first published on 5 February 2015 as *ISEAS Perspective* 2015/6.

he remains under a lot of influence from party politicians — particularly Megawati (chairwoman of the Indonesian Democratic Party Struggle) and Surya Paloh (chairman of National Democratic Party).

HOLDING A MINORITY GOVERNMENT AGAINST CRISIS-RIDDEN OPPOSITION

With only 37 per cent seats in the parliament, Jokowi's Great Indonesia coalition (comprised of PDI-P/Indonesian Democratic Party – Struggle, Partai Nasdem/National Democratic Party, PKB/National Awakening Party, and Hanura/People's Conscience Party) has an uphill task in passing their policies. After all, 2014 saw by far the most polarizing elections being held in Indonesia, and there is still a big divide between both candidates' camps — which has extended into the parliament where Jokowi leads a minority government against a much bigger Red and White Coalition (consisting of Partai Gerindra/Great Indonesian Movement Party, Partai Golkar/Functional Group Party, PKS/Prosperous Justice Party, PAN/ National Mandate Party, and PPP/United Development Party), led by Prabowo.

The divide between Prabowo's supporters and Jokowi's have created splits even within individual parties, notably the PPP and Golkar. These have manifested as leadership crises that have left the two major parties in tatters. The crisis in PPP had been obvious since the presidential campaign period when Suryadharma Ali's personal move to endorse Prabowo was rejected as the party's official position. The party currently has two chairmen. Suryadharma is chairman of the PPP camp that staunchly supports Prabowo, while Romahurmuziy controls the faction that favours Jokowi.

It is a different story with Golkar, as neither Aburizal Bakrie and Agung Laksono — the two leaders who claim legitimate leadership — are acknowledged by the government. Aburizal is adamant about Golkar staying with Prabowo, while Agung is sympathetic to Jokowi. Golkar, which was once the political vehicle of Suharto's New Order, is a more intricate case given its size and reach. Nonetheless, with both PPP and Golkar undergoing crisis, the strength and effectiveness of the Red and White Coalition has been seriously compromised.

Meanwhile, former president Susilo Bambang Yudhoyono's Democratic Party has been playing both sides. While claiming neutrality, it leaned towards Prabowo during the campaign. The defining moment came with the move of the opposition to support the abolishment of direct local elections, one of the most important achievements of Indonesia's democratic reform. SBY first claimed his firm support for the indirect mechanism, but his party then staged a walk-out in the voting process ensuring the return to indirect method. Wishing to leave behind a legacy of a democratic president, SBY demonstrated determination to defend the direct election and salvaged his reputation by issuing Perppu (government regulations in lieu of law) in a bid to annul the controversial laws. Partially thanks to the weight of SBY's political lobby, the Perppu was passed in January 2015 under Jokowi's administration and SBY thus dodged the indirect pilkada becoming his legacy.

Coupled with the leadership crises in the opposition, the passing of the Perppu has put the opposition on the defensive — giving Jokowi a window of opportunity to push reforms through. How long this situation will last however, and whether the government would have to pay back either the Democratic Party or the opposition for the Perppu deal in the future, is uncertain.

MAJOR APPOINTMENTS: THE POLITICS OF PLEASING AND APPEASING

The timing of the cabinet line-up announcement, which came later than promised had caused concerns about what went on behind the scenes. It became clear later that the delay in announcement was mostly due to intense negotiations with various parties and the involvement of the KPK (Komisi Pemberantasan Korupsi/Corruption Eradication Commission) in vetting the candidates. While trying to sway the opposition by offering seats, Jokowi needed to repay supporters within his own coalition for their support during the campaign. Still, even the vetting could not prevent some disappointment with the line-up. Here it must be noted that, despite vowing not to follow the usual practice of giving cabinet posts as rewards, it was the only realistic option for Jokowi — both to minimize the resistance he knew he would face in the parliament and to please his supporting parties. As such, Jokowi tried to strike a complicated balance between the credible individuals in the line-up, and those that may be appointed for other reasons.

On the positive side, the cabinet has many credible reformists, such as Anies Baswedan (Minister of Culture and Primary and Secondary Education, famous for an innovative programme on education), Ignasius Jonan (Transportation Minister, who successfully rejuvenated the state's rail system as president director of state railway company Kereta Api Indonesia, or KAI), and Lukman Hakim Saifuddin (Minister for Religious Affairs, a renowned progressive moderate Muslim). The minister that has attracted most attention however, is Susi Pudjiastuti (Minister for Maritime Affairs and Fisheries, a successful entrepreneur), who defies conventional stereotypes of a senior policy-maker. However it is her policies that have attracted a lot of interest, such as her strong call to beef up security in Indonesian waters, which was followed by the destroying of illegal fishing boats from neighbouring countries.

On the negative side, some posts were given to questionable individuals such as Megawati's daughter Puan Maharani (Coordinating Minister for Human Development and Culture) who severely lacks experience in government, and many of the ministers were clearly appointed to reward their parties, such as Siti Nurbaya Bakar (Minister for Environment, Nasdem Party) and Imam Nahrawi (Minister for Youth and Sports, PKB). At the same time, Rini Soemarno (Minister for State-Owned Corporations) who is known as Megawati's close aide faces questions about her involvement in corruption cases. The appointment of Defence Minister Ryamizard Ryacudu has also raised some eyebrows over his track record in human rights abuses.

The bid for inclusivity for all ethnicities can also be seen in the appointment of an Acehnese, Sofyan Djalil (Coordinating Minister for Economics), and a Papuan — Yohana Yambise (Minister of Women Empowerment and Child Protection). Another appointment which fulfilled both party and expert elements was Manpower Minister Hanif Dhakiri who is an activist not only in PKB but also on labour issues.

The pressure to please parties and supporters is apparent in Jokowi's choices for other important positions. The appointment of Luhut Panjaitan — Jokowi's close aide and long-term business partner — as presidential chief of staff, resembles another done as a reward. Nevertheless, the former general should prove a capable official in this position. Prasetyo, a Nasdem Party cadre with a questionable track record in prosecuting major drug and terrorism cases — was smoothly appointed as attorney general.[1]

WHEN PLEASING AND APPEASING BECAME PERILOUS

Jokowi's latest move to nominate Budi Gunawan as National Police Chief has been the most controversial. Not only was Budi the sole nominee for the position, the KPK had apparently questioned the size of his bank account in 2010 and had warned Jokowi already when Budi was being considered as a ministerial candidate. The KPK move to declare him a suspect a day before he was to be interviewed by the parliament shocked many, and there are numerous speculations about Megawati being behind Budi's sole nomination. He was after all Mega's adjutant. There are also views being expressed that Jokowi made the nomination to appease Mega but then allows the KPK to take the necessary action against the man. That way, Jokowi keeps his hands clean.

What has become clear is that this appointment has deteriorated to a conflict between PDIP and the police on one side, and the KPK on the other. Initially, a PDIP official Hasto Kristiyanto accused KPK's chief Abraham Samad of once lobbying party executives to support his bid to become the running mate of then presidential candidate Jokowi, and that Budi has now been named a corruption suspect because he was instrumental in spoiling Abraham's lobby.[2] The sudden arrest on 23 January by the police of Bambang Widjojanto, another chief of KPK, has elevated this issue to a conflict between the police which is long reputed to be one of the most corrupt institutions in the country and Jokowi's own PDIP, against the KPK — the anti-corruption agency with an excellent track record. The arrest was based on a report from an untrustworthy PDIP politician, and although Bambang was quickly released, it is apparent that the KPK has been targeted as its other leaders have also been reported to the police. This has presented Jokowi with yet another conflict, where he needs to take action and yet weigh the party support he needs with his focus on good independent government. While there is hope that the independent committee that he has set up to investigate and settle the matter may be effective,[3] he himself may do better in restoring public's faith by being more directly involved.

Complications aside, Jokowi has clearly given the appointees the mandate to work. Consequently, many of ministers have made important breakthroughs. Other than Susi's no- nonsense approach for her portfolio, Anies has worked hard on the long-mismanaged school curriculum, while the discourse for more flexibility and better working conditions showed the Manpower Minister at work as well. The mandate has also been accompanied by threats, that if any of them failed to achieve the targets set for them (the Ministry of Agriculture for instance is required to return Indonesia to rice self-sufficiency within three years[4]), Jokowi will not be reluctant to replace them. It is also clear however, that pleasing and appeasing has come at a cost of integrity for the president.

THE IMPORTANT TESTS: FUEL PRICES AND DISASTER MANAGEMENT

The decision to increase fuel prices was never going to be easy. Jokowi used his honeymoon period's momentum to do that and was fortunate to have the expected inflation dampened by the international drop in oil price. While former president SBY had been reluctant to cut oil subsidies, Jokowi did so within one month after taking office. The policy could save the 2015 state budget around Rp120 trillion (US$9.8 billion) — funds which Jokowi wants channelled to his various reform programmes. The drop in crude oil price has made it possible to completely lift the subsidy. In an unprecedented move, the government has also decided to reduce fuel prices accordingly and leave them to fluctuate.

To have a better control on this valuable resource, the government has also moved to pursue what is known as Mafia Migas or Oil and Gas Mafia, referring to certain groups who control the pricing and purchasing procedures of oil and gas in Indonesia with the aim of retaining a large personal cut. Such large-scale corruption has cost the state an exorbitant amount over the years, and the Energy and Mineral Resource Ministry has set up an independence team to provide specific recommendations to increase transparency and improvement management of these resources. So far, the team, led by economist and outspoken critic Faisal Basri, has been hard at work. For once, there seems to be some hope for improvement in this sector — although real results still seem a long way away.

At the end of 2014, the crash of Air Asia Surabaya-Singapore flight QZ8501 presented a test of disaster management. The accident put a spotlight on some of the serious problems in Indonesian aviation. There is lax control which had allowed a flight without permission to fly to take-off; and the pilot allegedly did not have the latest weather update before flying (investigation is on-going, but weather seems to be a major factor in the crash). Indonesian authorities quickly moved to suspend the air controller in charge of permitting the airplane to fly, and making obligatory for airline to brief pilots on the latest weather update, as well as investigating other airlines which may have disregarded specific regulations on their slotted flying time(s). While it is clear that Indonesia needs to step up regulation to keep up with the increasing demand of air travel, overall the management of this disaster has highlighted the solid work of the government's machinery as well as good cooperation with neighbouring countries. The National Search and Rescue Agency (Basarnas) and the Indonesian Navy in particular, have been working relentlessly to locate the plane and to recover and return the bodies to the grieving families.

CONCLUDING REMARKS: CONFIDENCE CORRODED

The first few months of Jokowi's presidency point to some efforts to overturn his doubters who perceived him as indecisive. To some extent, he has managed to do so by the quick decision to increase the fuel price and lift the subsidy, the hardline approach on sinking illegal fishing boats, and the denial of clemency for foreign convicted drug traffickers.

However, what he needs to focus on is to earn back some of his lost credentials. The current delay in Budi's inauguration, the ruthless action of the police in the arrest of Bambang Widjojanto, and his hesitation to take actions against the relentless attacks being ensued against the KPK, have deteriorated the public's confidence in him. His efforts to build a capable administration will be a waste if he cannot maintain some independence as a president and escape his current position as a hostage — most probably at the cost of the support of parties, quite possibly even his own. His latest move in approaching Prabowo seems like a desperate attempt to source for a different support, which has the potential of costing him more. To tackle the main problem which is the attack against KPK, Jokowi needs to acknowledge that Indonesians trust the KPK much more than the police, which means that he may have to abandon party support to maintain public faith. Put simply, he needs to take a side. Jokowi simply cannot afford to compromise further, not after such a hype in his inauguration and not after proving he can be a capable and determined leader.

Notes

1. Rendi A. Witular, "Mediocrity, controversy shroud Attorney General Prasetyo", *Jakarta Post*, 21 November 2014 <http://www.thejakartapost.com/news/2014/11/21/mediocrity-controversy- shroud-attorney-general-prasetyo.html>.
2. Hans Nicholas Jong and Ina Parlina, "PDI-P launches reckless attack on KPK boss", *Jakarta Post*, 23 January 2015 <http://www.thejakartapost.com/news/2015/01/23/pdi-p-launches-reckless-attack-kpk-boss.html>.
3. "Jokowi Bikin Tim, Ada 7 Keanehan Kasus Bambang KPK", 26 January 2015 <http://www.tempo.co/read/news/2015/01/26/063637613/Jokowi-Bikin-Tim-Ada-7-Keanehan-Kasus-Bambang-KPK>.
4. "Jokowi: Tiga Tahun Belum Swasembada, Saya Ganti Menteri Pertanian", *Kompas*, 10 Desember 2014 <http://bisniskeuangan.kompas.com/read/2014/12/10/121200526/Jokowi.Tiga.Tahun.Belum.Swasembada.Saya.Ganti.Menteri.Pertanian>, see also Harwanto Bimo Pratomo, "Jokowi: Menteri tak capai target langsung ganti", *merdeka.com*, 7 November 2014 <http://www.merdeka.com/uang/jokowi- menteri-tak-capai-target-langsung-ganti.html>.